/11/93    /10/03

✓ current ed 4/01

# THE FALKLAND ISLANDS

# Other Books by Barry Gough

# The Falkland Islands/ Malvinas

## The Contest for Empire in the South Atlantic

BARRY GOUGH

THE ATHLONE PRESS
London and Atlantic Highlands, NJ

First published 1992 by
THE ATHLONE PRESS LTD
1 Park Drive, London, NW11 7SG
and 165 First Avenue, Atlantic Highlands, NJ 07716

*British Library Cataloguing in Publication Data*
A catalogue record for this book is available
from the British Library

ISBN 0 485 11419 4

*Library of Congress Cataloging in Publication Data*

Gough, Barry M.
    The Falkland Islands/Malvinas : the conquest for empire in the
South Atlantic / Barry Gough.
        p.  cm.
    Includes bibliographical references (p.    ) and index.
    ISBN 0 485 11419 4 (cloth)
    1. Falkland Islands—History.  2. Argentina—Foreign relations—
—Great Britain.  3. Great Britain—Foreign relations—Argentina.
I. Title.
F3031.G68  1992                                               92-21952
    997'.11—dc20                                                   CIP

Typeset by Blackpool Typesetting Services Ltd, Blackpool
Printed and bound in Great Britain by
The University Press, Cambridge

# Contents

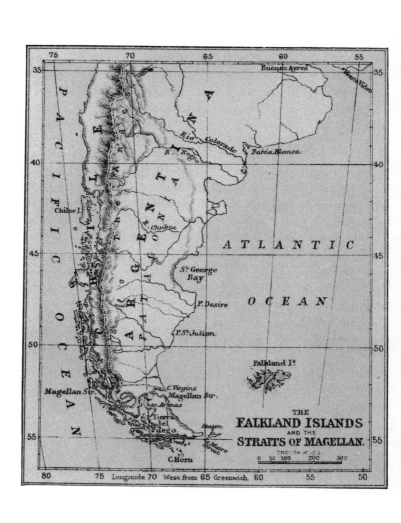

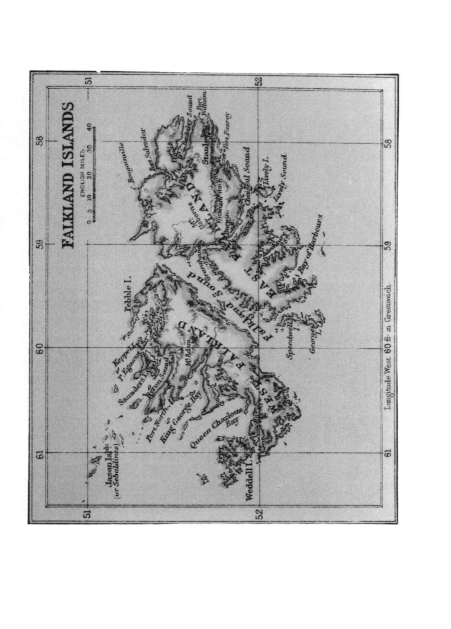

FALKLAND ISLANDS

ENGLISH MILES.

0 5 10 20 30 40

Maps reproduced from
CP Lucas *A Historical Geography of the British Colonies Vol II*
*The West Indies* (2nd ed. Oxford: Clarendon Press, 1905)

*To*
*Spencer John Gough*
*and*
*Zachary Samuel Morris Gough*

To proportion the eagerness of contest to its importance seems too hard a task for human wisdom. The pride of wit has kept ages busy in the discussion of useless questions, and the pride of power has destroyed armies to gain or to keep unprofitable possessions.

Not many years have passed since the cruelties of war were filling the world with terror and with sorrow; rage was at last appeased, or strength exhausted, and to the harassed nations peace was restored, with its pleasures and its benefits. Of this state all felt the happiness, and all implored the continuance; but what continuance of happiness can be expected, when the whole system of European empire can be in danger of a new concussion, by a contention for a few spots of earth, which in the deserts of the ocean, had almost escaped human notice, and which, if they had not happened to make a sea-mark, had perhaps never had a name?

Fortune often delights to dignify what nature has neglected, and that renown which cannot be claimed by intrinsic excellence or greatness, is sometimes derived from unexpected accidents. The Rubicon was ennobled by the passage of Caesar, and the time is now come when Falkland's Islands demand their historian.

Samuel Johnson, LL.d., *Thoughts on the Late Transactions Respecting Falkland's Islands* (1771).

# Preface

This is a book concerning a complex and, at times, tragic series of events over three centuries in the distant, wind-swept reaches of the South Atlantic. Long before the 1982 war that area of the world witnessed deep-seated rivalries and hostilities which have been lost sight of in more pressing events of our own era. Now, ten years after the Anglo-Argentine war, a fresh look is demanded of historical causes not diminished by the accretions of time.

This work belongs to several interlocking categories of historical inquiry. I should like to classify it as what is now called International History, for it is a five-sided study of Spanish, French, British, American and Argentine aspirations and enterprises in regards to the Falklands Islands or Las Islas Malvinas. It is also an assessment of British decision-making in the era of *Pax Britannica* and a contribution to the literature of British naval, imperial and colonial history.

'A morsel of rock that lies somewhere at the very bottom of America' is what the English satirist Horace Walpole called the Falkland Islands in 1770. How curious it was, he remarked to a friend, that two civilized nations, Britain and Spain, should be quarelling about this distant spot. Could not they find something nearer to fight about, he asked? 'Next century I suppose we shall fight for the

Dog Star and the Great Bear.' His contemporary, Dr. Samuel Johnson, also wondered why England and her rival should be in contention 'for a few spots of earth, which, in the deserts of the ocean had almost escaped human notice.'

More than two hundred years later the British are still directing their energies to the maintenance of sovereignty over the Falkland Islands. No longer is their rival Spain, but Spain's legatee to claims in the southern reaches of the Atlantic Ocean, Argentina. The actors have been replaced. But the conflicting sovereignties have changed hardly at all. And the answer to 'Who owns the Falkland Islands?' is found only in the records of history and the successes of occupations.

I request the reader to note that in this work the place-names the Falklands Islands and the Malvinas are used interchangeably and without prejudice to the claims to sovereignty of either the United Kingdom or Argentina. The prevalence in the text of the appelation the Falklands, or Falkland Islands, is merely a representation of the currency of that term in English and American sources. The term Malvinas, as will be explained, derives from ancient usage in first French as Les Malouines and then Spanish sources as Las Malvinas, and the latter is common today. That a war is waged to the present day as to which is the correct name to give these islands is symbolic of the larger question of the disputed sovereignty of the archipelgo.

I have not sought to explain, or to judge, the legitimacy of the claims of either party in the ongoing dispute. What I have sought to recreate and make sense of is the motivations of the various parties and the particulars of the events of times past, especially for the century or so beginning with the earliest occupation and colonization of these islands. As will be seen, the contestants have legitimate claims to pre-eminence of their claims. Put differently, as an historian I have not sought the unenviable role as sitting as international court judge. Rather, I have sought an explanation as to the origins of a deep-seated conflict, one that may possibly have additional chapters in the historical record as the perplexities of the present unfold into the mysteries of the future.

The sources for this study are numerous, rich and varied, and a full list is to be found at the back of the book. The work is heavily based in British primary documents, as will be seen in the end notes. The principal collections are in Admiralty files, Foreign Office papers and Colonial Office correspondence. I have not been able to travel to Argentina for the purpose of gathering documentation in the national archives; instead I have had to be content with using Argentine documents found in the diplomatic correspondence of the British Foreign Office and among the files gathered in the mid-nineteenth century by the British consul in Buenos Aires, Woodbine Parish. Additional primary material concerning the Argentine history of the Malvinas is to be found in the papers of the United States' Secretary of State, available in printed form. In respect of historical studies Rear-Admiral Laurio Destéfani's highly important 1982 book on the history of the Malvinas is the standard contemporary work, and I have relied upon it extensively. Julius Goebel Jr.'s and W.C. Down's studies on the Falklands story in international law, Hoffmann and Hoffmann's more recent perspective on international law and politics, and Anthony B. Dickinson's economic history of the Falklands constitute companion works to my own, stressing as they do aspects of the subject which enlarge our understanding of its complexities. Among numerous studies of the 1982 conflict, in historical perspective, Peter Beck's trenchant, no-nonsense *The Falkland Islands as an International Problem* is highly recommended as are articles by Guillermo Makin, Peter Calvert, Denzil Dunnett, Peter Beck and Lawrence Freedman in *International Affairs* 59, 3 (Summer 1983).

It would be quite misleading to advise the reader that a full account of all the historical particulars of the Falklands/

Malvinas saga will be found in this inquiry. But I would make the point that this is the first examination to employ all known primary historical materials of the subject, more especially the British reoccupation in 1832 and 1833, the naval activities of the British in those seas in the nineteenth century, the relationship of the oft-forgotten American actions to those of Argentina and the United Kingdom, and the various British schemes to defend or colonize the islands in the mid-nineteenth century. Although the British have been frequently classified as hard-nosed and heavy-handed in their imperial activities, it will be shown from this probe into the past that their motivations were not always clear and that their progress was often faltering. Fear of losing preeminence seems to have lain at the root of their actions, an historical force of great significance but sadly little appreciated in the annals of human activity. Equally conspicuous in the Argentine sources is the sense of outrage. Such response is completely legitimate, more especially as the Argentine government and their licensed and commissioned officers were sole, indeed successful, proprietors of the Malvinas at a time when the British government gave no attention to islands that they chose to neglect as irrelevant to their progress and prosperity. Historians of the 'end of empire' wrote their books too soon; historians of decolonization ought to rethink their fundamental premise. They wished for something which the past could not surrender: legacies.

For the student of British naval and imperial history this subject offers many opportunities, for the work embraces the era of the old colonial system, the changing circumstances of the so-called Second British Empire, and the complexities of decolonization. An assessment of the Falkland/Malvinas issue in relation to British expansion, consolidation, and, to a lesser degree, contraction, is to be found in the concluding chapter.

Some years ago a preliminary version of the main theme

of this work was presented to a meeting of the Imperial History Seminar in the Institute of Historical Research, London University, and I am grateful to Glyndwr Williams, P.J. Marshall, Andrew Porter and others for their comments and perspectives. Portions of this work have appeared in the scholarly journals *ALBION* and *The American Neptune*, and I record my thanks to the respective editors, Michael J. Moore and Timothy Runyan, for allowing reproduction here.

I record my gratefulness to a number of libraries and institutions that have assisted with my research. I thank the librarians and staffs of the Public Record Office, Kew and Chancery Lane, London, the British Library Manuscripts Department, the National Maritime Museum, the Cambridge University Library, the Scott Polar Research Institute in Cambridge, the Royal Geographical Society, the Athenaeum, the Royal Society, the Hydrographic Department, Ministry of Defence (Navy), Taunton, and Mystic Seaport, Connecticut. Permission to quote from the manuscripts of the Public Record Office is by courtesy of the Crown Patents Office. I acknowledge, with thanks, the permission of the Trustees of the Broadlands Archives Trust to consult and quote from the Palmerston Papers held in the Historical Manuscripts Commission, Chancery Lane, and the permission of the Trustees of the British Library to quote from the Woodbine Parish Papers and the Earl of Aberdeen's Papers. Peter N. Davies, Martin Lynn, Christon Archer, John Morris, Marilyn Morris, Neville Thompson, Bernard Stonehouse and Suzanne von Harpe provided encouragement. My university, Wilfrid Laurier, provided a publication subvention and a constant commitment to scholarly research endeavours, and I thank Barry McPherson, Noni Coleman, Evelyn Jones and particularly, Elsie Grogan for assistance. The Laurier Centre for Military, Strategic and Disarmament Studies made a grant in aid of publication, and I record my thanks to Professor

Terry Copp the Director. A number of persons have read sections of this work while it was in preparation, and I am particularly obliged to Andrew David for hydrographical details, to Henry Ferns, Helen Wallis, Ann Shirley, Richard Herr, Fernando Monge Martínez and Manuel Moreno Alonso for advice, to John Bockstoce for leads on Stonington sealing vessels, and especially to Robert Headland for details of various voyages to the Southern Ocean. Errors of fact and interpretation remain mine alone.

# CHAPTER 1

# Prologue:
# The Key to the Pacific

By geographer's computation, the group of islands known as the Falklands or Malvinas in the South Atlantic, excluding their dependencies,[1] lie in 51 to 53 degrees south of the equator and in 57 to 62 degrees west of the prime meridian. By surveyor's reckoning, they cover 4,618 square miles of land. By geologist's report, they constitute part of the South American continent, connected by a submarine plateau linking them to the nearest point in Patagonia, 250 miles distant. They lie 300 miles northeast of the Strait of Magellan and a thousand miles south from Montevideo and Buenos Aires. They number about two hundred but generally can be counted as two main islands, West Falkland and East Falkland, around which cluster smaller ones of various size. These are generally divided by Falkland Sound, a narrow strait running northeast to southwest and nowhere more than twenty-two miles wide.

On the northern coast of the western island known as West Falkland are numerous entrances from the sea, but the principal one leads to a small, sheltered sheet of water called Port Egmont. In clear weather, the access to Port Egmont is visible from a considerable distance at sea, and in favourable conditions it could be sailed into without risk[2]. Port Egmont led to Saunders Island. Here the ruins of the first British settlement in the Falklands, founded in 1766, still stand on the south side of a mountain which rises not less than six hundred feet above the level of the sea. The town was called Ford George, and sometimes mistakenly, Fort St. George. But whether named for England's king or England's patron saint, it was British in origin. Against the relentless opposition of nature the settlers had extended their gardens to the westwards of this mountain. Parsley and celery grew well. Fresh drinking was there for the taking. One observer remarked that the country appeared capable of cultivation, fine peaty soil lay in the ravines, and grass appeared plentiful.[3] The island abounded in wildfowl – geese and snipe particularly – and rabbits. Fish were easily caught. There was an abundance of excellent peat, too. Nowhere, however, could one see a tree. Solitude reigned supreme.

'I tarry in this unhappy desert,' remarked the pious Father Sebastian Villanueva in 1767, 'suffering everything for the love of God.'[4] The good priest had every reason to complain about life in the newly-settled Spanish colony on East Falkland Island. The place was windswept and bleak, rocky and boggy. No trees afforded shelter from the incessant winds. Deposits of peat provided the only available fuel. The climate was cold and boisterous, and in winter very wet. Of this place and this priest, it has been written by Julius Goebel, Jr., with true understanding, 'Little wonder that these islands should have been the last of the great discoveries in the West to be settled by Europeans, and that only the love for one's country or one's God could persuade men to remain in the face of such an unfriendly nature.'[5] The chronicle of human endeavours in this South Atlantic home of rock and water is one of hardship, shipwreck, suffering, and loneliness. The rigours of the South Atlantic delayed discovery and slowed progress.

In these unpleasant circumstances, as Goebel put it, 'none but the more intrepid navigators who sought a direct passage westward to the rich lands of the East ventured southward, and they, indeed, lingered no longer than they were obliged to.'[6]

The Falkland Islands or Las Islas Malvinas emerged from the mists of time in the age of reconaissance. Who first discovered them remains uncertain but the claim most probably goes to John Davis of Devon. In 1592, having failed to find a northwest passage to Cathay via the strait that bears his name, Davis had sailed as an associate of Thomas Cavendish in the expedition to the 'backside of America' to find the western entrance to the Arctic seaway. On 14 August, after a heavy storm, Davis put into the islands for protection. Davis claimed the islands were never before discovered. He was too distressed to make any particular observations about these islands; nor did he even give them a name. Eighteen months later, Sir Richard Hawkins made a further exploration, and named them Hawkins's Maiden Land in honour of his queen and to perpetuate his own memory. In 1600 the northwestern extremities were sighted by the Dutch navigator Sebald de Weert and named the Sebaldines. Thereafter, 'Haukinsland,' as the Dutch also called the place for some years, saw few mariners. English attention was drawn to Magellan's Straits and to Patagonia, while most seaborne trade to eastern seas passed by way of the Cape of Good Hope. In 1690 the English captain John Strong, sporting a letter of marque from William and Mary, landed, and named them 'the Falklands Islands,' after Viscount Falkland, then Treasurer of the Navy. Thereafter, for a considerable period, they stood alone. 'We scarce hear anything more of these islands for near a century,' remarked the chronicler of the *Annual Register* for the year 1771, 'so that even their existence has been called in question.'[7]

Such early probes as had been undertaken by the English

into the Pacific Ocean and to the western shores of the
Americas were concocted from imperial motives that were
discursive and designed to counter Spanish hegemony.
Until the mid-eighteenth century, it must be remembered,
Britain enjoyed no dominating position in world affairs,
no ability to dictate or even suggest to her rivals that
which British statesmen and strategists preferred as a
logical course of action to increase the power and prestige
of the nation. In disadvantageous circumstances, English
activities were, more often than not, fitful, opportunistic
and adventurous. They showed no grand design, except to
pick away at Spanish power as circumstances offered.
Englishmen, as has been often said, were late starters in the
growth of maritime empires, and although they confined
their initial activities to various seaborne trades, to
government-sanctioned forms of merchant venturing, and
to colonial schemes in North America they always cast a
longing glance at 'the wealth of the Indies' and the treasure
fleets that crossed the ocean each year, enriching Spain in
so many enviable ways.

To tap the wealth of the Spanish empire lingered as a
theme in English activities. Accordingly, the West Indies
and Caribbean became the cockpit of English action, and
here smugglers, privateers and other interlopers struck at
Spanish supremacy, breaching, whenever they could, the
wall of prohibition and restriction erected to isolate Spanish
American trade from any and all rivals. A secondary and far
larger field of action lay in the southern reaches of the
South Atlantic and on the remote but vulnerable Pacific
shores of Chile, Peru and Panama, and even as far north as
Mexico. English ships sailed into the South Seas in order to
penetrate the defences of the Spanish empire, and only after
the mid-eighteenth century did any disinterested zeal for
exploration motivate the crown to undertake official expeditions. For the time being, English projects and ventures
into South America and the Pacific were unauthorized,

though English statesmen watched their progress with hopeful anticipation and not a little financial interest.[8]

The Pacific exploits of Francis Drake, Thomas Cavendish and Sir Richard Hawkins constituted the first phase of English activities on the west coasts of Spanish America. In 1669, however, a fresh impulse appeared in the form of a voyage undertaken by a naval officer, John Narborough, in the vessel *Sweepstakes*. Narborough carried instructions from the Duke of York, the Lord High Admiral, stating that the design of the voyage on which he was employed was to make a discovery both of the seas and coasts of that part of the world, and, if possible, to lay the foundations of a trade there. The English captain entered the Strait of Magellan and completed a trustworthy survey of the famed waterway. He then sailed to Valdivia in Chile. He had imagined that he could incite the local natives to throw off the yoke of the Spanish rulers, but in this he was mistaken and misguided, and the local authorities seized four men and put a stop to this expedition of transparent motives. The English government took no notice of the voyage or of Narborough's persistent pronouncements of how a new world of advantageous trade might be established in those parts. As the mariner had learned to his cost, the Spanish government would only admit foreign traders if forced to do so.[9]

For some decades after Narborough's voyage, English interest in this region remained sporadic. The lure of gold baited a pack of English buccaneers, including Captain Morgan, John Strong, and William Dampier. They fell upon Spanish towns and ships in any way they could manage, and they described their achievements in fast-selling narratives. Such reports made good copy. Daniel Defoe, the journalist and author, picked up on the theme of lucrative maritime war against a wealthy, vulnerable Spanish America. To him may be ascribed the honour of having proposed, to government, the planting of a pair of

English settlements, one on the coast between the Rio de la Plata and the Strait of Magellan and the other on the Pacific Coast, at Valdivia or Coquimbo farther north. The British government took no direct, immediate action, while during these same early decades of the eighteenth century the French, against similar odds, carried a trade into the South Sea and sold goods to the Spanish, to the growing disappointment of English policymakers. Still, the illusion remained. In 1711 the British government chartered the South Sea Company to encourage the nation's trade beyond Cape Horn; however, the whole South Sea project, designed to float the national debt, and open business with Spanish America was a fiasco. In fact, more was gained by the nation in arms during the war with Spain, ending in 1713, than by all the musings of the commercial imperialists. At the peace England extracted from her former enemy that which rival France had so dearly prized, the slave *asiento* or license for a period of thirty years. Thus, for the very first time, a legal form of British trade with Spanish America had been secured. A chink had been made in the Iberian armour.

The outbreak of war with Spain in 1739 brought forth what has been described as 'a flood of schemes for the exploitation, occupation or even dismemberment of Spain's colonial empire.'[10] National policy aimed at avoiding entanglement on the European continent; at the same time there was a tendency to look to seaborne means of cutting away at Spain's dominance. In the Admiralty office originated a scheme that resembled the old piratical strikes – the conquering of Chile, the plundering of Lima, the attacking of Panama and even, if circumstances warranted, the establishing of British rule at Lima if the locals appeared disposed to the liberators. To these aims was added another: seizing of Manila in the Philippines, the Spanish haven that was the destination of the fabulous Acapulco galleon. Commodore George Anson, R.N., was given command of the expedition. The exploits of the squadron exceeded all expectations, and Anson's ship, the *Centurion*, returned to England with colossal treasure.[11]

Accounts of this voyage, particularly the official account, published in 1748, urged that the Falklands should be surveyed, and that this should be done as a preliminary step towards the establishment of a British base near the Cape Horn entrance to the Pacific. Anson never saw the Falklands. However, he had a keen eye to strategic advantage. Moreover, he had become well aware of the possibilities for commercial growth and imperial ascendancy in the South Seas. In consequence, his recognition of the strategic position of the Falklands, often quoted, gave immediate credibility to all such previous geopolitical musings by Defoe and others. Immediately, the Admiralty laid plans for an expedition of reconnaissance. British claims that this was a scientific pursuit did not fool the Spanish, who protested at the obvious nature of foreign encroachment. The Spanish minister Carvajal made abundantly clear to the British ambassador Keene that 'he hoped we would consider what air it would have in the world to see us planted directly against the mouth of the Straits of Magellan, ready upon all occasions to enter into the South Seas.'[12] Sensing the diplomatic consequences of the situation, and the degree of Spanish anxieties, the British government cancelled the proposed expedition. Once again, plans for distant ventures were altered, even delayed, by international requirements nearer home. Again, the old problem asserted itself, as an English statesman put it in 1711: 'the prospects of opening a new trade with the Spaniards and of attacking their colonies at the same time tended to be repugnant to one another.'[13] The English government had not yet developed the maxim of the nineteenth century – trading to Spanish America on equal terms with all powers – and for the moment Spanish policy remained exclusionist, despite growing difficulties within the empire.

Even so, British power relative to that of France and Spain was changing quickly. British interest in the Pacific became truly oceanic and increasingly commercial and was erected on the framework of the years before 1763 and the sporadic activities of English adventurers beyond Cape Horn. 'In the second half of the century,' Glyndwr Williams has written, 'British interest in the Pacific was to be at once wider and deeper . . . attention turned to unknown areas rather than to settled coasts; the insistent quest for knowledge became a motive as important as more material considerations.'[14] The Anglo-Spanish rivalry for the Falklands was a key episode in the new phase of rivalry that followed the end of the Seven Years' War. As with the British capture of Manila in 1762, James Cook's explorations of the Pacific beginning in 1768, the search for new markets and bases, the commercial enterprises of mariners, and the successes of British merchants in Spanish America in consequence of the upheavals of the Napoleonic Wars, the contest for the Falklands demonstrated that the era of the informal agents of imperialism was giving way to that of state-engineered expansion.

For some time the Falklands were forgotten or neglected. This was so until, as Dr. Johnson puts it in his *Thoughts on the Late Transactions Respecting Falkland's Islands* 'the conduct of naval affairs was intrusted to the Earl of Egmont, a man whose mind was vigorous and ardent, whose knowledge was extensive, and whose designs were magnificent; but who had somewhat vitiated his judgement by too much indulgence of romantic projects and any speculations.' Egmont saw the Falklands as a subject for bettering national security and by enhancing British prospects in the distant oceans. His 'eagerness after something new,' as Johnson terms it, was not the propelling factor. As the preamble to Captain Byron's secret instructions attest, the advancement of trade was the long-range objective of his voyage, and with opulence came defence: '. . . nothing can rebound more to the honor of this Nation as a Maritime Power, to the dignity of the Crown of Great Britain, and to the advancement of the Trade and Navigation thereof, than to make Discoveries of Countries hitherto unknown, and to attain a perfect Knowledge of distant parts of the British Empire . . .' – these words indicate the preeminence of trade over discovery, of the need to create, as Professor Harlow states, 'a network of commercial exchange extending through the Pacific and Indian Oceans.' Egmont's scheme was no idle speculation but a conscious revival and reassertion of ambitions dating from the national policy of Elizabeth.[15]

On 18 June 1764, Commodore the Hon. John Byron, R.N., in command of the frigate *Dolphin* and the sloop *Tamar* sailed from Plymouth Sound under a cloak of secrecy so as not to invite Spanish suspicion and reprisal. The ships' destination had been announced publicly as the China Seas. In actuality, the expedition's objects were to explore the South Atlantic Ocean and to lay claim to the harbour of Port Egmont and all neighbouring islands under the name of the Falkland Islands for King George III and, once that was accomplished, to sail north beyond California and find the western entrance to the supposed Northwest Passage. On 12 January Byron dropped anchor in one of the finest harbours – capacious and safe – and he named it Port Egmont after the Earl of Egmont, the first Lord of the Admiralty. 'I took possession of this Harbour and all these Islands for His Majesty King George the Third of Great Britain and His Heirs,' recorded 'Foulweather Jack' Byron in his journal, to which he added laconically, 'tho' they had been before taken Possession of by Sir Richard Hawkins in the Year 1593'.[16] The hoisting of British colours on shore, the saluting by three guns from the *Dolphin*, and the serving of half an allowance of brandy to every man in order to drink the king's health completed the day.[17] Byron examined the island cluster, coasted the shores of East Falkland discovered by the Dutch navigator Roggeveen in 1721, and gave Berkeley Sound its name. Had he taken pains to penetrate its entrance a few miles he would have come across, to his undoubted surprise, a thriving French settlement, recently commenced, known as Fort Saint Louis and founded by Bougainville. The motivation of the British government in sending Byron to take the Falklands was to fulfill a perceived need, announced by the chaplain of Commodore George Anson's *Centurion* in consequence of the 1740–44 circumnavigation, of establishing 'a convenient station situated so far to the southward, and so near Cape Horn.' Such a base in time of peace would be 'of great consequence to the nation' while 'in time of war would make us masters of those seas.'[18]

Byron, like Lord Anson before him, became convinced of the fundamental value of the Falkland Islands to British naval preeminence. 'The whole navy of England,' he had written with unbridled enthusiasm of Port Egmont, 'might ride here in perfect security from all winds.'[19] There was good water and good soil, advantages in themselves. Nothing was wanting but wood.

At the Admiralty, the Earl of Egmont became convinced that 'this Station' was *'undoubtedly the Key to the whole Pacifick Ocean.'* and for emphasis underlined *it* thusly in his letter to his cabinet colleague the Duke of Grafton, the Secretary of State. 'This Island,' stated Egmont in belief of the western island's geographical utility and unbounded prospects

> must command the Ports & Trade of Chile, Peru, Panama, Acapulco, and in a word all the Spanish Territory upon that sea. It will render all Our Expeditions to those parts most lucrative to Ourselves, most fatal to Spain and no longer formidable, tedious or uncertain in a future War. And the coast of Chili from

the Straights of Magellan to the Isles of Chiloé being wholly Savage, uninhabited by the Spaniards, and possessed by the most warlike of all native Indians in perpetual Hostility with Spain. The country is abounding above all the rest in mines of Gold and Silver, and the Navigation thro those Straights from this Island to Chiloé being now well known, and such as will seldom exceed a Month.[20]

To Egmont's way of thinking, the nation that should 'first fix a firm footing there' would make prodigious gains and outdistance all rivals.

The enterprising Egmont instructed his secretary, Henry S. Conway, to draw up a long memorandum for government detailing a proposal for a surveying and colonizing expedition. Three vessels – a frigate, a sloop and a store ship, all well-manned and fully-provisioned – would take a pre-framed blockhouse and a Royal Marine detachment of twenty-five men from England to Port Egmont. There they would complete Byron's work, secure British dominion, enhance the British claim, and forestall the French, whose very presence in the South Atlantic though not then known was anticipated.[21] Egmont was extremely serious about this project, even to the degree of bypassing the cabinet, of lobbying the King, and of actually resigning because the Duke of Grafton and other cabinet colleagues prevaricated before the expedition was finally directed to proceed.[22] Egmont's enthusiasm had two results. It led to Captain John McBride, R.N., being commissioned to survey and settle the Falkland Islands, and it led to Captain Samuel Wallis in the *Dolphin* and Captain Philip Carteret in the *Swallow* being sent to find the southern continent thought to lie somewhere in the watery wastes between Magellan Strait and New Zealand.

Obedient to his instructions, McBride in the frigate *Jason*, accompanied by the sloop *Carcass* and the storeship

*Experiment*, proceeded to Port Egmont. On Saunders Island McBride planted gardens. 'We are endeavouring to make Gardens,' he had written home to Lord Egmont but cautioned: 'my Expectations of them are not sanguine. This country, I believe, must have abler Farmers than Sailors to make anything of it.' In his view, ships destined for the South Seas and calling at the Falkland Islands for supplies really would be obliged to rely for refreshment upon 'what Nature has thrown upon them.'[23] That meant the humble and monotonous table offerings of geese, snipe and even wild celery. McBride fared better in various construction projects: his men erected a battery mounting eight guns, they made a wharf for the convenience of ships taking in water, and they put up two houses. In all, this afforded modest shelter but was nonetheless home for the British Empire's most southerly possession. The garrison was now kept, McBride said trenchantly, 'shrinking from the blast, and shuddering at the billows.' 'We supposed,' McBride wrote in terms far less laudatory than Commodore Byron's and with considerable mirth 'that we should be permitted to reside in Falkland's Islands the undisputed lords of tempest-beaten barrenness.'[24]

McBride's mission evidenced a guarded imperial intent on behalf of Britain against any rivals. His instructions empowered him to force any 'lawless' person to take the oath of allegiance to H.M. government or to leave. In the eventuality that any foreign settlement be found, the inhabitants were to be told that the islands were under British sovereignty; such squatters were given six months in which to leave. If they lacked their own transport they were to be taken off in H.M. ships and, while on board, 'treated with all tenderness and care.' The government did not want an international incident over such persons, and in the eventuality that they would not leave peaceably and took no notice of the warning one of the British warships was to sail for home to report on the state of affairs. In the eventuality that a foreign settlement were found at Port Egmont the inhabitants were to be warned off. But McBride was to avoid hostilities and could only effect a joint occupation. He was not to grab a bit of empire for his sovereign and hold it against all odds: any dispute about sovereignty was to be settled by the home government and the representatives of other crowns.

Such carefully crafted instructions stood the British captain in good stead. In these seemingly remote islands the British garrison was not alone. In looking around the heights of the adjacent islands, McBride discovered in a bottle the distressing and unwelcome evidence, as he reported in taciturn tones to the Secretary of the Admiralty, that 'other Frenchmen had lately been here'.[25] A scout sent to reconnoitre confirmed McBride's worst fears: the French had taken up residence in Berkeley Sound and had been in undisputed possession of the place for nearly three years. McBride sailed there in the *Jason*. He protested to the French commandant, M. de Nerville, that his settlement was illegal. The French officer was not to be intimidated, being (as he was) in possession of a commission from His Most Catholic Majesty. Not only did he refuse; he threatened war if the British landed forces. McBride, pursuant to his instructions, withdrew from the scene, thinking it better not to resort to arms. A return to a general war which pitted Britain against an alliance of France and Spain was altogether unthinkable. The mettle of the French had been tested.

How did the French come to be there? French ambitions towards the world overseas also took on new proportions in the mid-eighteenth century, particularly in consequence of the Seven Years' War. This conflict, truly global, exhausted France financially and threatened her continental preeminence. New France and India had been lost to British arms. The French marine was in near ruins. Many French politicians and patriots regarded the new circumstances as degrading and dangerous. The peace established in 1763 was temporary, and the likelihood of a return to global warfare exceedingly high. In these disadvantageous conditions, strategic planning was necessary, and preparing for armed struggle mandatory. By occupying unsettled territories a gain could be made on British ambitions and provide a counterweight to the probable enemy's anchors of empire. In these ways, too, new bases would take the place of old ones lost. This policy was made even more desirable by the restricted opportunities for trade in the Indian Ocean and by the closing of French immigration to Canada. By virtue of the fact that government was in no position to carry out any schemes it fell to individuals to undertake enterprises by any means they might see fit to enhance their nation's power and prestige. The expedition of Bougainville and the French colonization of the Falklands stems directly from this situation.[26]

Louis-Antoine de Bougainville, soldier and sailor, knew firsthand of the disasters that had befallen France in Canada. He knew, too, of the loss of empire in India and the Antilles. The terms of the Treaty of Paris in 1763 constituted, to his way of thinking, the birth certificate of English world power.[27] He looked for ways to rebuild the colonial and maritime edifice of a France that lay in ruins, and he determined to erect a new one. Gains in the northern hemisphere seemed closed to France. The South Seas, thought to be limitlessly profitable, and a new seat of empire, remained unclaimed by the covetous English, concluded Bougainville. He knew Admiral Lord Anson had advised his government to take immediate possession of the Falklands. He perceived that peace would not afford the English with an interlude for idleness in their designs. 'What interest should the English have in doing otherwise,' he wrote in his diary, 'than secure, in the interval such as the present, a base which at first sign of another war would place them in the position of the arbiters of

Europe?'[28] He concluded that a march must be stolen on them, and he conceived a scheme to go and plant the fleur-de-lys on the Falklands.

Bougainville now brought the scheme before King Louis XV, who warmly embraced it but sadly could offer no state financial support. The entrepreneur did obtain His Majesty's royal warrant, quite necessary in the circumstances, for empire on the loose, one quite unauthorized, was not to Bougainville's liking. The Falklands enterprise was from beginning to end a seaborne operation, too, and Bougainville exchanged his rank of colonel in the army for that of captain in the navy. As for the requisite monies, he turned to his family's fortunes, particularly that of an unwary uncle. Adequately funded, he journeyed from Paris to St. Malo where he sought out local shipowners and builders, particularly M. Duclos-Guyot, who constructed and armed the frigate *Aigle*, mounting 20 guns, and the sloop *Sphinx*, 12 guns. At St. Malo, also, he engaged mariners for the enterprise. Nearby he met with three families of Acadians who had relocated in Britanny after their land had passed into British hands during the recent war. He promised to transport them to a country where he would endow them with lands, and to encourage their loyalty and patriotism he gave them advances of money and goods. This was the forward party. They sailed in September via Brazil and Montevideo, and five months later, on 3 February 1764, they landed in the Falklands to found a new corner of French empire.[29]

Bougainville's survey of the islands was hardly encouraging. 'A landscape bounded on the horizon by bleak mountains,' he recorded in his notebook, 'the foreground eroded by the sea which seems to be ever struggling for supremacy; a country lifeless for want of inhabitants; neither pasturelands nor forests for the encouragement of those who are destined to become the first colonists; a vast silence, broken only by the occasional cry of a sea-monster; everywhere a weird and melancholy uniformity.'[30] This was not a moment for the fainthearted. 'An agony of homesickness clutched at their hearts in those first hours of contact with this distant land, lost in the ocean,' remarks Bougainville's biographer, 'but though at first it seemed an impossible place for the establishment of a colony little by little hope revived.'[31] They discovered waterfalls and rivers, extensive pastures, numerous living creatures, antiscorbutics and some combustible materials. Wood was scarce. The shores of the bay were covered by a thick grass eighteen inches long. The fishing was wonderful and sea-lions and seals were abundant, promising oil. Penguins, 'like choirboys in surplus,' said Bougainville, were numerous.[32] No fierce animals or venomous reptiles presented themselves. Wildfowl were abundant. The sky was clear, the climate mild. The reality of it all exceeded the colonists' every expectation.

The French commander took his time to select a place for his fort. He needed a secure emplacement adjacent to a snug harbour. He chose a spot at the head of a bay, along a small natural harbour, connected with the open South Atlantic by a narrow channel. Earthworks to mount fourteen cannon were built. Huts for the colonists and sheds for provisions were constructed. The fort, once completed, was christened Fort St. Louis, and a twenty-foot obelisk was raised in the centre of the little citadel sporting a sculptured fleur-de-lys and two plaques, one showing the king, the other the arms of France. In the presence of the *habitants*, officers, men and seamen Bougainville unveiled a monument to France's newest colony. 'Vive le roi!' was shouted and a twenty-one-gun salute followed. Bougainville displayed the royal patent appointing the governor of this new colony and he presented it to his cousin M. de Nerville, who had helped to finance the expedition. On 5 April 1764, Bougainville took formal possession in the name of the king; three days later he sailed for France in the *Aigle*.[33]

Once back at court Bougainville could confirm his proceedings and obtain royal support. His frigate was refitted and sailed, again with Bougainville in command, for the Falklands, this time with 53 new colonists. At Port Louis he found the colony prospering. The heifers and horses brought from France on the first voyage were in good health. Plants and vegetable seeds introduced from Europe did well in the new environment too. The commandant reported his complete contentment with the colony's affairs except for the scarcity of wood. Bougainville steered for Magellan Straits to rectify this deficiency. In the dreaded straits the navigator chanced upon the ships of Commodore Byron. From the English Bougainville learned that Byron had also come from the Falklands, from a place he had called Port Egmont, known to the Frenchmen as Port de la Croissade. Bougainville dismissed the English claim as untenable, for Byron had left no colonists to ensure dominion. The following year, 1766, the British government sent out colonists. Meanwhile, Bougainville returned to the Falklands with timber having, as he expressed it, 'opened up a seaway necessary for the support of the colony.'[34] A month later he sailed again, this time for France, with knowledge that he had established a firm footing of dominion in the South Atlantic. He had no idea that 'international' politics were to wield a dreadful blow to his schemes.

Bougainville's scheme spelled trouble – for Britain, for Spain, for France and for himself. As the historian of French exploration in the Pacific states: 'he had indeed stirred a hornet's nest'.[35] 'At first,' writes Professor John Dunmore, 'the French were unwilling to sacrifice so easily a settlement that held such interesting possibilities. But to hold on to the Falklands would definitely mean alienating Spain, and possibly lead to a new war with England – for which France was prepared neither militarily nor morally. Pressure was therefore put on Bougainville to abandon the settlement and recognize the Spanish claim.'[36] Bougainville himself went to Madrid and conducted negotiations on the matter with the French ambassador and the Spanish ministry. Nothing could be done. However, were Bougainville to agree to withdraw his settlement, thus enabling France to recognize Spain's right to the Malouines, the royal Bourbon ranks of the two crowns could be closed and the British case weakened.[37] In the view of Professor Dunmore: 'Right of ownership by prior discovery was the only claim the British could fall back on, once the French had admitted that their own early settlement infringed Spanish sovereignty. And ownership by mere discovery was not a principle the British were anxious to establish in international law.'[38] The French king was sympathetic, and he offered Bougainville the governorship of Mauritius and Bourbon, but the entrepreneur had his heart set on a voyage of discovery around the world; accordingly, the French government outfitted an expedition to advance discoveries in the South Seas. The Spanish government, for its part, refunded Bougainville's financial investment plus five percent interest (£24,000 in those days), assuming as they were the equipment, supplies and establishment at Port St. Louis.

Bougainville was handsomely indemnified for his labour and, ever loyal to his monarch, undertook the last duty in the islands – officially transferring the colony to the Spanish. Bougainville was appointed to the command of the frigate *Boudeuse* and sailed under instructions for Rio de la Plata where he was to meet with two Spanish men-of-war, sail together to Port Saint Louis, undertake the transfer and then, alone, sail to the South Pacific on further discoveries and complete, for the very first time, a French circumnavigation.[39]

The Spanish standard was hoisted on 1 April 1767 succeeding the white flag of France. The 150 inhabitants who greeted their returning patron learned the king of France's pleasure: they could remain in the islands under Spanish rule or they could, with the administrative staff, take their leave of the place, sail for Montevideo in the Spanish ships, and make their way home.[40] A few families remained but most took their leave of the place. Some men joined Bougainville's expedition as sailors. The French occupation of the Falklands, les Malouines, had terminated.

Spain's reaction to French encroachment had been mild indeed and certainly moreso than that against Britain. The reason was well stated by the principal French minister, the Duc de Choiseul, when he confessed, somewhat later, that there was hardly the same 'reason for jealousy... as there would naturally be with a power so formidable at sea as England was.'[41]

Now Spain's ministers had become awakened to the realities of British expansion in the South Atlantic. Not only did they learn of McBride's settlement and survey. They had found out from Bougainville that the British were seeking to rectify their want of a refitting and replenishing station in those latitudes. Bougainville, a dutiful student of history, had told the Spanish ministry that Commodore Anson, on his return from his celebrated circumnavigation, had attributed his double failure to make a richer haul of Spanish prizes on the Pacific coast of the Americas and to foment a revolution there to one cardinal fact: the lack of a good base of supply near the Strait of Magellan where his vessels could refit.[42] What were the possibilities? What were the alternatives? Chiloé, the temperate, heavily-forested island in southern Chile, had commodious, safe anchorages quite different from gale-plagued Valparaiso farther north.[43] Farther again towards the Equator lay the Juan Fernández Islands, the largest being Más-a-Tierra, home of Alexander Selkirk, Defoe's Robinson Crusoe. Anson had been attracted to the Juan Fernández group, more particularly the larger island. But now it was manned by a Spanish garrison, and all further thoughts of an English occupation there were out of the question. Yet there still lingered the need for a southern seabase, and as the Dutch navigator Roggeveen had trumpeted of Juan Fernández, whosoever should settle it could become the master of a country as wealthy as Mexico and Peru, or Brazil.[44]

As a British-controlled base on the searoad to the China Seas McBride's settlement at Port Egmont posed a singular threat to the Spanish Empire in the Americas. Situated strategically as a station from which armed ships could prey upon Spanish colonial ports and shipping in time of war, and from which merchant vessels could engage in illicit trade in time of peace, there seemed little doubt that in rival hands it could be extremely dangerous to an already over-extended Spanish authority.

Under royal order of 24 November 1766, Spain created the Governorship of the Malvinas, and placed the islands and their immediate waters under the jurisdiction of the nearest constituted authority, the Captain-General of Buenos Aires, Don Francisco Bucareli. Under this new arrangement Port Saint Louis acquired a new name, Puerto Soledad. And Bucareli's instructions were crystal-clear on the subject of interlopers:

> His Majesty [wrote Burcareli's superior on 25 February 1768] orders me to charge you that no English establishments are to be permitted, and you are to expel by force any already set up if they do not obey the warnings, in conformity with the law. You need no other orders nor instructions, and in observing these measures you will consider nothing except your own troops and those of the occupants in order that you do not expose yourself in case of inferiority to failure. In such a case or in anticipation of other bad consequences which your excellency can deduce from the state of the province you will resort to protests and accusations declaring that no action will be

taken until the king has been informed and his orders received.[45]

The British lingered at Port Egmont in tantalizingly close proximity to Spanish forces. From time to time, the Spanish harried the British colonists there and demanded their withdrawal. The British refused, and even issued their own threats. This cat-and-mouse affair was not to last long. In January 1770 two Spanish men-of-war touched at Port Egmont and found it occupied. Their officers discovered the interlopers and repaired to the Viceroy with the fresh, alarming news.

On 6 May a hefty Spanish expedition under Don Juan Ignacio Madariaga, consisting of a squadron of five frigates bearing 1600 troops, sailed from Buenos Aires, for Port Egmont with orders to dislodge the English establishment there. The Spanish commander landed his troops on 10 June and opened a musket fire on the blockhouse. The British post was stoutly defended by Captain George Farmer, R.N., who commanded the garrison. Farmer had refused to believe that his Spanish opposite, Madariaga, would be foolish enough to risk the peace existing between the two powers.

Before long the defenders were obliged to surrender. Farmer's force could offer no sizeable resistance, and they capitulated and quit the islands under protest. The ejected settlers reached England in September 1770, a few weeks after news of the Spanish expedition's intention. In London the press, public and government regarded this high-handed expulsion as an outrage.

The Spanish ambassador in London seems to have been taken aback by the events in the South Atlantic and embarrassed by the surprising turn of events. He went to see the British Secretary of State, Viscount Weymouth, and confessed that he had good reason to believe that Viceroy Bucareli in Buenos Aires had taken it upon himself to use force at Port Egmont. Bucareli we now know as a tough-minded and heavy-handed administrator sent to clear out the Jesuit missions in Paraguay: in the Falklands he was taking measures to maintain the integrity of his sovereign's realms. Though he was obviously unmindful about the sensitivities of the Falklands/Malvinas issue, he was actually fulfilling his instructions of 1768 already cited. The Spanish ambassador was in the corner. He trusted that such an event would not endanger the good relations existing between his country and England. Weymouth could not agree to any of this. He pointed out that the British commandant's instructions called for pacific responses: to warn off subjects to other powers and to refer differences concerning the right of control to the respective sovereign. The British were on a collision course with this policy, a policy framed along most naive grounds. Poor Captain Farmer had been left out on a limb; now it was time to get him back. Very quickly, the government determined on a large naval armament, and they did so as a salutary reminder of what might transpire should Spain not show a suitable degree of accommodation to British diplomatic demands. The Secretary of State, Lord Weymouth, insisted on the immediate restoration of the colonists to Port Egmont; he also called for reparation for the insult offered to the British crown.[46] The Spanish government now appealed to France for assistance in virtue of the 'Family Compact,' and the French minister, Duc de Choiseul, endeavoured to mediate between the two countries along the lines of the previous arrangement between France and Spain. However, Louis XV of France, old and disillusioned, refused Spain, much to the disappointment of Choiseul who was anxious to regain French influence and had elaborated a scheme of naval renascence and diplomatic calculation. Louis dismissed Choiseul from his post and backed out of the dispute. Negotiations with Britain were resumed. Spain, left alone, surrendered to a scaled-down version of British contentions. Even so, Spanish claims to rights of sovereignty remained unrefuted. The Spanish had disavowed the 'violent enterprise' of Captain-General Bucareli in Buenos Aires in sending Don Madariaga's force, and had even been obliged to restore to Port Egmont all the stores and effects previously seized.

Under terms of the Declaration on 22 January 1771, the powers agreed Spain would make a complete restitution, but with a very specific reservation that the engagement 'to restore to His Britannic Majesty the possession of the fort and port called Egmont cannot nor ought any wise to affect the question of the prior right of the sovereignty of the Malvinas Islands, otherwise called Falkland Islands.'[47] In other words, the restitution did not preclude the claims to sovereignty by one or either of the powers; nor did it favour one claim over another. It recognized British possession and rights of occupation at Port Egmont.

To effect the restitutions, the Admiralty sent the frigate *Juno*, the sloop *Howard*, and the storeship *Florida* under command of Captain Stott to receive the possession of the Falklands in the King's name. On 13 September, Stott arrived at Port Egmont and the next morning, seeing Spanish colours flying, the troops on shore, he sent a lieutenant to inquire if any officer was empowered to make the restitution. The reply was that Don Francisco de Orduna, a lieutenant of the Royal artillery of Spain, was ready to do so and was so empowered. Captain Stott carried copies of the Spanish monarch's orders, and after delivering them to his Spanish counterpart, proceeded with his counterpart to examine the settlement and stores. On the 16th Stott landed with a party of marines and was received by the Spanish officer who formally restored Port Egmont to the British along with its fort and dependencies. By this the British were given the same possessions as before 10 June 1770. Stott caused the British colours to be hoisted. The next day Don Francisco with all the troops and subjects of

Spain sailed away in a schooner. But this was really a hollow display of British dominion in the South Atlantic. The government decided to scale-down its force to a small sloop with about fifth sailors and twenty-five marines on shore, under the belief that the force was so small that the Spanish would not think the British intended to annoy them.

By a secret, verbal undertaking which the king, George III, later confirmed in a conversation with the Spanish ambassador – but which has never been found in written form, despite various, repeated searches – the British had promised to withdraw their garrison from Port Egmont in due course. This, to the Spanish, had been part of the bargain, anxious as they were to halt a British station at the gateway to the South Seas. However, the British ministry, perhaps fearing political rivals at home, perhaps also worrying that the secret agreement might be disclosed, took no hasty action.[48] While the British dominion in the South Atlantic continued in a precarious state, in London Junius and Dr. Johnson engaged in a war of words that kept the British literate public bemused if not informed.

Then, as if in a sudden about-face, the government on the grounds of fiscal exigency, ordered the colony abandoned. Government instructed the officer commanding H.M.S. *Endeavour* to embark on board the garrison and all useful equipment and supplies, and to return them to Portsmouth. Some lasting reminder was to be left to indicate continued British ownership. Upon the sight of sail in Port Egmont the garrison was delighted that their term of duty had come to an end. To a man they rejoiced at the prospects of going home and of ending their desolate and estranged isolation. The least happy person in Port Egmont on 20 May 1774 was the commandant, Lieutenant S.W. Clayton, R.N., a keen naturalist and an energetic gardener. The fine shore establishment of Fort George had to be left behind. As the Surgeon's Mate Bernard Penrose recorded in sad solemnity: 'the glory of our Colony was the gardens, which we cultivated with the greatest care, as being fully convinced how much the comforts of our situation depended upon our being plentifully supplied with vegetables'.[49] And such a contrast these gardens were to the 'mountainous, boggy, rocky and everywhere barren' prospect of the Falklands, as Commandant Clayton remarked in his description of the place's natural history.[50] Left as sole sentinel at the settlement was a lead plate, affixed to the door of McBride's blockhouse. It bore this engraved inscription:

Be it known to all nations, that Falkland's Island, with this fort, the storehouses, wharfs, harbours, bays, and creeks thereunto belonging, are the sole right and property of His Most Sacred Majesty George the Third, King of Great Britain, France, and Ireland, Defender of the Faith, etc. In witness whereof this plate is set up, and His Britannic Majesty's colours left flying as a mark of possession by S.W. Clayton, Commanding Officer at Falkland's Island, A.D. 1774.[51]

That plaque was first taken by the Spanish to the Buenos Aires archives and then by the British general William Carr Beresford to England where its existence is not known.[52] As for Lieutenant Clayton, his proconsular duties were over. He had to content himself with admiring the Falklands flowering myrtle that he transplanted safely to his garden in Peckham, south London.

Even before the *Endeavour* reached Saunders Island with orders to evacuate Port Egmont, Spain's authorities in Buenos Aires had instructed the governor on the Malvinas that the King of Spain desired that 'you may consequently observe, with due prudence and caution, whether the English do, in fact, abandon the said settlement. . . .' He was further instructed to 'renew your exertions to make sure that they do not return to that quarter.'[53]

In obedience to these orders, Captain Juan Pascual Callejas visited Port Egmont. He found British whalers in the vicinity, and he thus advised his superiors of these intrusions. Although prohibitions were issued, the British vessels treated them as hollow and as of little legal consequence, and continued in their use of the Falklands. Meanwhile, the Spanish kept a sizeable garrison at Puerto Soledad. By 1785 that colony boasted a total of thirty-four buildings and upwards of one hundred residents, including the garrison. From time to time, too, the captains-general and, after 1775, their successors, the viceroys of Buenos Aires, sentenced criminals to lonely exile on the Malvinas. In addition, they authorized rather extensive marine surveys by Pablo de Zizur, Don Pedro Maza, and Don Jeronimo Loraton.[54] The Spanish clung grimly to the Falklands in the face of many difficulties. Not the least of these difficulties was the outbreak of a general war in Europe in which the Iberian peninsula became a principal battleground.

In these circumstances of British neglect and of Spanish ambition it was altogether appropriate that Spanish forces should take the opportunity to destroy the remnants of the settlement of Port Egmont. This they did in March 1780, six years after the British had left flag and plaque as fragile signs of ownership.[55] Acting on instructions from Madrid they demolished the settlement and left no trace of British occupation. The place was never again occupied.

In truth, Port Egmont never had much utility for British shipping but it grew as a symbol of past occupation for the British. As many British naval officers were to note in their reports of proceedings and in their own remark books, Port Egmont was a grand harbour and was safe to ships when they were once inside; however, it was ill-chosen, for it lay in an awkward western location, far off the usual track of oceanic shipping, especially for vessels homeward bound from the Pacific.[56] The Spanish never settled there, wisely preferring the more accessible Puerto Soledad, Bougainville's brilliant discovery of a suitable site of occupation in the island group. Yet the British, with bulldog persistence, never let their historic claims to Port Egmont or their voluntary withdrawal from the settlement of Fort George on Saunders Island in 1774 interfere with their larger claims to sovereignty of the Falklands. Port Egmont came to serve an altogether different purpose – a symbolic one – from that of its founding and occupation. For the British, the key to the whole Pacific Ocean acquired a new meaning as the anchor for British claims to the sovereignty of the Falklands.

# CHAPTER 2

# Trade, War and Revolution in the South Atlantic

The question of who held the sovereignty of the Falkland Islands, Las Islas Malvinas, was deeply rooted in the intricacies of International Law. To the west of the great line of demarcation, established by the papal bull *Inter caetera* of 1493 and enshrined by the Treaty of Tordesillas of the following year, Spanish dominion extended from the Cape Verde Islands half way round the world to and including the Philippines. Beyond that line, and stretching around the globe's other half, lay Portugal's mighty share – to and including Brazil. Thus the Falkland Islands and all of South America save Brazil fell within Spain's hemisphere. Subsequent to these international agreements both crowns had developed competing spheres of influence in South America.

The Spanish empire, with its highly centralized administration, ranks as an extraordinarily successful achievement in its own right and one of the greatest empires of all time. In spite of Spain's grim determination to maintain her imperial interests and national predominance, such a position of influence was not possible in an age of trade expansion, protracted war, and emergent revolution. This empire's collapse had telling consequences everywhere

that the great Iberian kingdom had sent forth its administrators and traders, its soldiers and priests.[1] Along the
lengthy coastline of South America smuggling against
imperial regulation was commonplace. Spain's laws
exacted stiff punishments against smugglers and pirates.
Even so, for the successful entrepreneurs the profits were
commensurate with the risks. The English were the most
irreverent traders in regard to Spanish regulation – and
'singeing the King of Spain's beard' was regarded by the
likes of the Grenvilles and the Drakes as good sport.
Spanish treasure ships, especially those homeward-bound
from the Caribbean, were always fair game.[2] So, too, on
the Pacific side of the Isthmus of Panama, was that
celebrated prize, the Manila galleon, which shaped an
annual passage to Acapulco from the Philippines and back.
The Falklands, lying conveniently off the continental
shore, afforded a choice lair for illicit traders working the
waterways of the South Atlantic. The French, especially
from Saint Malo, in the early eighteenth century refitted at
and sailed out of the Falklands. Indeed, they gave the
group the name *Les Iles Malouines*, corrupted by the Spanish
to *Las Islas Malvinas* – and from here the sailors of St. Malo
carried on their illicit commerce with Chile and Peru by
way of Cape Horn, and to a lesser degree with other ports
on the eastern coast.[3]

As noted, the first foreign legal commerce with Spanish
America was held by France under the *asiento*, of license.
But the constraining terms of it – one ship per year – only
served to encourage an enormous contraband trade.
England wrestled the *asiento* from France as one of the
spoils of the War of the Spanish Succession. Under the
terms of the Treaty of Utrecht, 1713, England's sole
annual ship to Spanish America (and that in the sordid
trade in slaves) was the first recognition of direct, legitimate Anglo-Spanish commercial interchange in the
western hemisphere. As the economy and population of

South America grew so did illicit commerce and the difficulties of Spanish attempts at control. And in due course, nascent nationalisms and revolutionary tendencies, fed by the successes of the American and French experiences, spread to Spanish America and to Portuguese-held Brazil. In these changing circumstances, forcing open the all but sealed doors to this rich continent remained a lingering English commercial dream.

Meanwhile, British seaborne commerce increased dramatically to eastern seas. India, China and southeast Asia bulked large as places of British activity, where competition with the French, Dutch and the Americans remained keen. Yet there were many other locales of significance, especially in relation to the history of the Falklands: the convict colony of Botany Bay, New South Wales; the sea-otter hunting base of Nootka Sound, Vancouver Island; the great trans-Pacific trading crossroads of the Sandwich or Hawaiian Islands; and, besides others, the Bonin Islands on the Siberian coast and the Marquesas in the South Pacific, both resorts for whalers. After the American Revolution, the Pacific Ocean witnessed a phenomenal exploitation by outsiders. New trades – in pelts and skins, in whale products, in timber and tea, and in hides and tallow – were pursued relentlessly by commercial interests from north-western Europe and the eastern North America. After 1815, oceanic commerce increasingly used the roaring 'forties. Cape Horn merchantmen shipped wool and oil from the Australian colonies, timber and flax from New Zealand, guano from the Chinchas, and nitrates and ores from the ports of Chile and Peru. The Royal Navy was making at least an annual freight in silver specie from shipment points as far north as the Gulf of California. In all these ways, the quickening pace of seaborne commerce was fulfilling promoters' promises of rich returns in the distant ocean. Such cargoes were invariably destined for ports in the North Atlantic. Equally significant, other cargoes, though of a more exotic nature, including sandal-wood, the sea slug *bêche-de-mere*, and edible birds nests, were shipped by European vessels in the Pacific to those celebrated entrepôts Canton and Macao, the gateways of business and diplomacy for the Chinese empire.

New England, or Yankee, ships were particularly active in this avenue of commerce, and for them the Falkland Islands also developed as a highly useful place of replenishment and refit. The American trader Edmund Fanning, for instance, advertized the Falkland Islands as a resort for Pacific and China voyagers. Ships would call to seek shelter, to make repairs, to gather driftwood for fuel, and to take on water. Wild hogs, which made excellent salt pork, and which were preferred by Fanning's crew over pork shipped from New York, could be easily got there. Geese, eggs, fish and game could provide a good sea stock, especially for ships outward bound to the Pacific. As for inbound ships, the Falkland Islands offered one last opportunity for whaling and sealing and for completing a cargo of skins. Seals from Falklands and nearby waters began to be commercially exploited during the last quarter of the eighteenth century, as whalers ranging the Southern Ocean came to realize that they could take on additional, profitable cargo. The fur seals, which they hunted for food and oil, were particularly valued for their luxuriant under-fur. The skins were shipped to Canton for clothing and to Britain and the United States for use in garment manu-facturing. Gradually a specialized industry in sealing developed. By the early nineteenth century this economy was to contribute mightily to that Anglo-American-Argentine rivalry which was to have such tragic propor-tions in the history of the Falkland Islands.[4]

So common did calling at the Falklands become in this age that accounts by mariners sailing to the Pacific seldom fail to mention the group. Some examples may suffice to illustrate this. The supercargo on board George Dixon's command, *The Queen Charlotte*, complained in 1786 when enroute to Nootka Sound, that the geese and ducks caught for food in the Falklands were 'exceedingly rank and filthy.' Still, he admitted that the crew's exercise in getting them was both agreeable and healthy.[5] Sometimes a vessel – witness the case of the Boston sloop *Union* – would put into the Falklands for food to save the crew from scurvy. Boat crews would scramble ashore and go after the profusely growing wild celery. They would raid rookeries of the penguin and the nests of the albatross.[6] They would hunt wild hogs – an easy task given the capabilities of a ship's dog, as in the case of the *Union*.[7] The crews of other vessels such as the Nantucket sealer *Washington*, Captain Jedediah Fitz, would plant potatoes, that 'very powerful antiscorbutic,' on the way outward bound to China, and harvest the crop on the way homeward.[8] Crews foraged for food and water everywhere they could – catching green turtles and hunting albatross. In cases of dire necessity, the Falkland Islands lay in a particularly convenient position for being touched at by ships outward or homeward bound on their long voyages, for almost invariably such ships were in need of a sea stock.

In addition, ships began to call in the Falkland Islands for the commercial possibilities of the islands themselves, and of the nearby seas which seemed bountiful in their resources. The key commodities were seal and whale products. Captain Fanning's pioneering successes en route to China led New England merchants to send out vessels specifically to engage in Falklands seal-hunting. [9] It is true that such vessels ranged widely to Kerguelen or Desolation Island, to the South Shetlands, to nearby Staten Island, and elsewhere. However, in the case of seal-skinner *States* owned by Madam Haley of Boston, she had been fitted out especially for the Falklands in search of fur-seal pelts and sea-elephant oil. It was a magnificent killing: she carried seal pelts to Canton where they each fetched a handsome price of between one and two Spanish dollars, then the standard trading currency there.[10] In the Falklands the captain had found it easiest to hunt the mammals by sending club-wielding boat parties to the beaches. There the seals, gathered in rookeries of four or five hundred in one contracted space, made the matter one of mere slaughter, especially as the seals could be easily approached.[11] In December, a preferred killing time, the seals were always on the beach in preparation for the birth of the young. The massive size of the herds indicated to the predators the prodigious possibilities of a supply without end. However, as one astute British observer noted with caution: 'There is no doubt that if this fishing was properly protected, it would become more productive; but several sealing vessels, particularly American, make a point of killing not only the full grown and legitimate game, but destroy a future chance by sacrificing the pups.'[12] Measures taken against these 'depredations' might be rewarding, it began to be reasoned. The Argentines were the first to argue in favour of conservation measures. Their government was the first to take up the challenge.

Other vessels came to the Falklands in the wake of the *States* and did so in rather increasing numbers. With a keen Yankee eye for economy, Fanning's *Volunteer* dropped off an officer and eight men at Port Louis, Berkeley Sound, deposited with them the frame and materials for a 30-ton vessel which they had brought from Sandy Hook, and left this party to take seals during the absence of the ship to the Pacific in search of sandalwood.[13] The commercial aspects of the voyage were in every way rewarding for this vessel: not only did the *Volunteer* take in a sizeable seal cargo, but she conducted a profitable trade at Coquimbo and other western ports in South America. This had political consequences, too. The *Volunteer's* captain, Fanning, found that other American vessels engaged in fishing, whaling and sealing had been detained by Chilean authorities for their infractions of local regulations. He made vigorous (and what turned out to be successful) appeals to the President of the United States, James Monroe, to send a U.S. vessel-of-war, the sloop *Ontario*, commanded by Captain James Biddle, round Cape Horn for the purpose of watching over American shipping in the Pacific, for transporting United States commissioners to Latin America capitals, and for planting the Stars and Stripes on the disputed banks of the Columbia River.[14] As for the Falklands' sealing industry, it was now reaching full flower under the aggressive American sea-hunters. During Fanning's first visit, in 1792, he counted some forty vessels, mainly of American and British registry, engaged in sealing in the Falklands. The industry was still carried on during his second visit, in 1798, but had expanded to Juan Fernández, to South Georgia, and to other southern islands. The sealers were a law unto themselves wherever they went. The slaughter they engaged in was wholesale and systematic, and the decline in stock was dramatic, to the point of extinction in all these locations by the 1830s. [15]

In these same years, specially-fitted ships scoured the Southern Ocean in pursuit of whales. Whale products were vitally, indeed strategically, important to the competing powers of the North Atlantic world. The British were early leaders in this field. But the French and Americans were pressing rivals. To maintain this ascendancy, the British government employed every known parliamentary and political stratagem in order to keep Nantucket whalers, the best in the business before 1776, within the lucrative fold of British mercantile regulation after the War of the American Revolution. In consequence, New Bedford in Nova Scotia, and New Haven in Wales, became new headquarters of the reorganized whale fishery. Healthy bounties authorized under the Acts of Trade and Navigation encouraged British whalers to range father afield into the Southern Ocean, despite increased inroads made by foreigners.

The British whaling interests – the Enderbys, the St. Barbes and the Campions – were keen ministerial and parliamentary lobbyists. They found a dutiful supporter in Charles Jenkinson (later Lord Hawkesbury and the first Earl of Liverpool), the President of the Board of Trade. Not only did the whaling lobby secure preferential duties of all favourable sorts. They were able to get the full support of government to mount an expedition in the early 1790s to examine the prospects of the Southern whale fishery and to investigate the possibilities for a site in the southern hemisphere for a base for British whalers. In keeping with Jenkinson's will, the British Admiralty in 1793 made available H.M.S. *Rattler* to the Enderby firm. As a merchant vessel she was commanded by Captain James Colnett, R.N., to sail to the South Atlantic and round Cape Horn. Her specific mission was to examine islands and harbours suitable for secure refitting and victualling stations 'for the purpose of extending the spermaceti whale fishery.' In the course of his reconaissance Captain Colnett had a good look at the Revilla Gigedo group lying south of Cape San Lucas, Baja California, Cocos Island off the coast of Central America, the Galapagos almost due west on the equator from Ecuador, and St. Ambrose and St. Felix Isles off the Chilean coast. However, he thought a base watched over by a British naval lieutenant should be established for the purpose of regulating the whale fishery. His alternative suggestions were Cape St. John, Staten Island, or the east end of the Falklands. Colnett's expedition highlighted the lingering needs of the British whaling industry for a snug base somewhere in the southern hemisphere. The British whaling interests continued to warn of Spanish settlements in Patagonia, and more particularly of the damage they could do to the British whalers, including driving British ships from their resort at the Falkland Islands. For the moment, however, the ministry took no action. The war with France commanded every attention, and no expropriation of territory took place in those seas.[16]

In these years of intermittent war and peace, British whalers ranged restlessly over the southern oceans. They pressed northwards into the North Pacific and Bering Sea, and in doing so employed Hawaii as their advanced base of operations.[17] This, too, enhanced the value of the Falklands: for the longer these voyages, the greater the need for places of repair and refit along the way. American and French vessels were equally active in the whale fishery, and even before the War of the American Revolution had commenced Lieutenant Clayton had given to London the warning that in the year 1776 ten North American vessels were profitably employed in the whale fishery in and near the Falkland Islands.[18] The abundant waters of Patagonia afforded a similarly favourite haunt, while whalers also scoured the shores of the Antartic continent. Some voyages, such as James Weddell's 1822-1824 expedition, drew attention to the possibilities of whaling and sealing in more southerly latitudes and further advertized the advantages of using the Falklands as a base for Antartic discoveries.[19] Others, such as Fanning's, broadcasted the attractive possibilities in waters of the Falklands themselves. At the south mouth of Falkland Sound, Fanning advised, whalers could be found in plenty. At nearby Arch and Eagle Islands good harbours existed where vessels might anchor and 'obtain cargoes of oil and bone, as fast as the oil can be tryed out.'[20] These indicated a growing industry of great possibilities, while the historians of the trade demonstrate the increased activity of the whalers to the mid-century, and an American ascendancy.[21] And at the risk of repetition, year-round whaling in southern waters enhanced the utility of the Falklands as a place of refuge, repair, recreation, rest and replenishment.

During the War of 1812, the Falklands took on a new and strategically important value, as did other island groups such as the Marquesas. From these lairs American privateers and naval vessels prowled the oceans and preyed on the large British whaling fleet. The U.S. frigate *Essex*, Captain David Porter, roamed almost at will in this easy work, that is, until the Royal Navy's small squadron under command of Captain James Hillyar of H.M.S. *Phoebe* finally trapped the *Essex* in a neutral port, Valparaiso, and defeated her when she set to sea.[22] The British also watched the Americans at one of their favourite haunts, Tristan da Cunha, off which in 1815 H.M. brig *Penguin* was obliged to strike her colours to the U.S. sloop-of-war *Hornet*. British naval officers also kept a steady eye on the enemy's movements in Canton, in Hawaii, in the Marquesas, and, not least, in the Falklands. The enemy's possession of the Falkland Islands, or any other base in southern waters, would add to their strength. Rumours persisted of foreign use of the Falklands. In 1813, for instance, it was believed mistakenly that four French frigates carrying 250 troops each were to rendezvous with a U.S. frigate and storeship in the Falklands before sailing to attack the British in their distant colony of Port Jackson, New South Wales.[23]

Thoughts of establishing a naval station in the Falklands did not linger in the minds of British policy makers. The reasons for this are clear. On either side of the South American continent the British had virtually unrestricted access to two great shipping and trading ports – Rio de Janeiro in Brazil and Valparaiso in Chile. It is true that each had its disadvantages, and Admiralty in-letters bulge with complaints by admirals and commodores of various abuses, and often indignities, they had suffered at the hands of local officials. There were additional problems. Rio's port duties seemed exorbitant. Valparaiso appeared in a state of perpetual civil war. Even so, in both locations food and water were always readily available, and the anchorages were reasonably safe, except in Valparaiso in the season of the great winds known as the 'northers'.

Early on in the history of British maritime endeavours in distant seas these great ports had demonstrated their value to Britannia. The Royal Navy had been using Rio de Janeiro as a naval base from 1777 and Valparaiso from the first decade of the 1800s. Rio, according to one historian, was England's most important non-European naval facility. It constituted the staging area for campaigns against Spanish American colonies and as well as a convenient fitting-out station for expanding trade with Asia and the South Pacific.[24] And at Rio, especially, the Royal Navy and the British government were almost always treated agreeably, if formally, by the host authorities – in itself no unimportant matter to British aims and decorum.

From these early years the obligations of the Royal Navy in South American waters had grown inordinately during the turbulent years of liberation and revolution. By 1808 the Admiralty was forced to meet these extended duties there and in the Pacific by establishing a new command – its South American, or, as it was dubbed, 'Brazils' station. By virtue of the constant turmoil of insurrection, revolution and civil war, and of Britain's anxiety to prevent any foreign intervention or Spanish repossession of lost colonies, the command constituted a challenging, problematic and important one, calling for a cool head, abundant awareness, and characteristic tact. When Rear-Admiral Sir Robert Otway accepted the command in 1826, his friend, the future King William IV, wrote to him: 'the appointment to the command in South America is, I trust, acceptable to you. Under the very extraordinary situation of those countries off which you will have to cruise, the command cannot fail to be interesting; and I rejoice that so cool and valuable an officer as yourself has been selected for this singular and special purpose.'[25] If the requirements of the station were great, the resources of the squadron were skimpy. Here as elsewhere during the years of *Pax Britannica* requirements invariably exceeded resources. The Brazils squadron usually consisted of a ship-of-the-line as flagship, a few frigates, a handful of corvettes and sloops, a couple of brigs, and a ketch or two. Considering that these ten or twelve men–of–war had to service the eastern Pacific as well as the South Atlantic they constituted a very meagre force, taxed to the limit. In response to growing British political and commercial interests beyond the Horn the Pacific became a separate command in 1837. But until that time the squadron's units were distributed, in the words of one British naval officer who knew these waters well, 'at those points where the presence of a British authority was most essentially required,' that is, besides Rio de Janeiro they were at Buenos Aires, Valparaiso, Callao, and San Blas on the distant, west coast of Mexico.[26]

Of all these seaports, Rio de Janeiro ranked as the key in these early years of revolution and transition. For although Spain's links with Spanish America were severed after Napoleon invaded the Iberian Peninsula, Portugal main-tained communications with Brazil by virtue of the Anglo-Portuguese alliance and British supremacy at sea. In 1807 the Portuguese royal family had removed to Brazil – in British warships – when France invaded Portugal. Brazil became independent in 1822 under Dom Pedro I, and Britain facilitated the recognition of the new nation by Portugal. British policy also endeavoured to restrain Por-tuguese actions in the northern and eastern flank of the Rio de la Plata known as the Banda Oriental, and to check the Brazilian slave trade. Otherwise, her object was to secure British commerce and to contain and defeat Napoleon and his ally Spain.[27]

Among competing loyalties in Latin America, commanders-in-chief and officers commanding Royal Navy vessels had to act with the greatest degree of circum-spection. Contending parties in areas such as the Rio de la Plata vied bitterly for preeminence. The Portuguese had a settlement at Colonia. Montevideo and Buenos Aires competed as rivals in the hide and beef export trades, and kept equally watchful eyes on the interior provinces to the north drained by the Paraná River. The French and Americans were aggressive trading rivals here, too. It took adroit diplomacy, remarked Rear-Admiral Sir Manley Dixon in praise of Commodore William Boyles in 1814, for the maintenance of friendly relations with 'the heads of the contending parties on each bank of the river; a relationship not very easy to maintain without having had a due observance to that system of neutrality, which has been so strongly recommended (by government) and so successfully adhered to.'[28] The British government posed no obligations of territorial acquisition on the Royal Navy, except in regards to the Falklands. Only in dire necessity would a landing party be sent ashore – to secure a bank's assets or to protect a customs house from any local interference. Generally speaking, the Navy confined itself almost solely to doing what it could do effectively, that is, 'to check piracy, protect trade, prevent the abuse of the right of blockade and keep any acquisitive European power from intervening.'[29] As long as Britain held preeminence at sea during the wars of liberation of Spanish America, Spain had no good chance of reasserting her former authority. Meanwhile, provided local governments were in agreement, the whole continent lay open to commercial penetration by the British, the Americans, the French, and others.

To this 'hands-off' or 'non-intervention' policy of the British government there was but one major exception. This episode in the history of British arms proved to be a hard-learned lesson for government about either authorizing an expedition to occupy any territory on the South American mainland or, once committed to the project, maintaining an army of occupation in the face of determined local revolutionary forces. The background to this

expedition – which led to the attempted occupation of
Buenos Aires in 1806 and Montevideo in 1807 – begins
with the strategic value of the Cape of Good Hope. This
'tavern of the two oceans,' as the Dutch affectionately
dubbed it, was a valued possession for merchant enterprise
in eastern seas.[30] From the British government's view-
point a weakened Holland could not be judged as capable
of holding it given Napoleon's designs on India. Commodore John Blankett put it particularly well when he
advised his superiors to consider the matter in not one but
two ways: 'first how it would suit us and then how it
would annoy us in other hands.' The Cape, he warned,
was but a mere feather in the hands of Holland; however,
it might become a sword in the hands of France. [31] Thus
the British, who had occupied the Cape in 1795 only to
return it to the Dutch in 1803 took it again in 1806 to
secure the sea communications to India. This time the
British kept it. Their motivation mirrored the opinion of
men in government that the Cape was 'the key to Asia' and
'the Gibraltar of the Indian Ocean.'[32] Did not Britain
already control the 'keys' to the Atlantic and Mediterranean oceans – Gibraltar, Malta, Bermuda, and others
besides? Britain must now possess the Cape and dominate
adjacent seas. Sir John Barrow, Admiralty secretary,
shared the view that the Cape would give Britain not only
a lever in eastern trade and security; it would have advantages in South American commerce as well, for it was conveniently situated as a base for an extensive trade which
might be opened with the coast of Brazil and the ports of
South America.[33]

The design for occupation of the Rio de la Plata owed its
origins to Commodore Sir Home Riggs Popham, R.N., and
at first it was unauthorized by and unknown to the home
government.[34] Popham was a restless officer who early in
his career had gained favour in high places.[35] Popham
determined, on the basis of advice from an American

seacaptain named Waine, that an occupation of the Rio de la Plata could be made, especially as the inhabitants of Montevideo and Buenos Aires were waiting, Waine claimed, to throw off the weight of Spanish tyranny and hold their cities for British trade. [36] Major-General Sir David Baird, who had commanded the land force that took Cape Town, possessed discretionary powers to send troops on to India if necessary. However troops were not needed there, and Popham knew of the long-standing interest his friend William Pitt, the Prime Minister, held in occupying the Rio de la Plata.[37] Popham possessed orders to cruise along the southeast coast of South America, but he had none authorizing him to land an army. At the Cape he was able to get Baird's consent, and he notified London of his intentions. Distance from London meant that waiting for a reply was out of the question, and Popham's squadron sailed from the Cape for the Rio de la Plata with a regiment of Highland Light Infantry, four guns, and some dragoons. In charge of the forces was Brigadier William Carr Beresford. En route, at St Helena, Popham convinced the governor to lend a 400-man local defence force, and they resumed their course for the South American coast.

In mid-June the squadron arrived in the River and troops were landed near Buenos Aires. Spanish troops made a stern resistance. For a time, Beresford and the 1,300-men army were held in check by local forces, and all Popham could do was establish a blockade and await reinforcements from England. The landing force, under Lieutenant-General John Whitelock, was defeated by Spanish troops under General Santiago de Liniers, who had help from local *patricios* to evict the foreigners. In these confused circumstances Whitelock withdrew from the two cities, leaving behind 1,676 British prisoners, an act which brought forth the indignation of the remaining troops-in-arms. Thus ended the British occupation of the Rio de la

Plata. As for the local patriots, Manuel Belgrano, one of the most famous, played a dominant role in the May Revolution of 1810, fought in Paraguay where he found the locals wanted independence but not Buenos Aires domination, and, most importantly, on 27 February 1812, unfurled a blue and white banner, the flag of the patriots. Subsequently he fought numerous campaigns, and he was prominent in convincing the Congress of Tucuman to adopt a declaration of independence and a flag, which they did on 9 July and 25 July 1816 respectively.[38]

Meanwhile, a change had come over the waters. Trade was one thing, dominion another. Popham's adventure embarrassed the government. Nevertheless, Whitehall had sanctioned the expedition once begun and instead of ordering a safe withdrawal had sent reinforcements.[39] In the future it was to be 'hands off'.[40] Assisting in a revolution and of throwing off the Spanish yoke had been demonstrated as hazardous and only possible with a great commitment of arms and a large loss of life. Sir John Fortescue, the distinguished historian of the British Army, goes even further: 'It was worth the humiliation, the loss of brave men and the expense of money to be freed once for all from the fatal entanglement of a permanent and precarious occupation of the Rio de la Plata.'[41]

In consequence of this episode, the British cabinet developed a clear-cut policy towards Latin America. This made absolutely certain that British aims should be the pursuit of trade and investment, not the increase of territorial control and obligation. Viscount Castlereagh, the Secretary of State for Foreign Affairs, drafted a memorandum for his colleagues in 1807 on the new policy to be pursued in regard to South America. He rejected all thoughts of British territorial acquisition; he rejected any intention to interfere in local politics; and he rejected all views of exclusive British political influence. On the contrary, he wrote, in guidelines that became Foreign Office dictum: 'the particular

interest which we should be understood alone to propose
to ourselves (in the context of the war with Napoleon)
should be the depriving our enemy of one of his chief
resources, and the opening of our manufactures the
markets of that great Continent.' In the words of Professor
D.C.M. Platt, '*Equality of treatment was all that was asked.*'[42]
And, commercial treaties, designed to open Latin American markets to all traders, did not give Britain preferential
treatment, only the possibility of competing with rivals.
British statesmen such as Castlereagh's successor George
Canning continued this 'hands-off' policy. They realized
that any high-minded attempts at stabilizing governments
or regimes would only lead to perpetual obligations of
difficulty.[43] But whether it was serving as umpire
between contesting countries over border disputes or as
bond-guarantor to a faltering government the British
government kept to the rule of non-intervention, making
infractions of it only at their peril. When they attempted
coercion of local governments 'in support of British
interests' they got their hands burned – as another foreign
secretary, Lord Aberdeen, learned painfully in the Rio de la
Plata in 1845, when attempting to assist Montevideo's
independence and safeguard British trade in the face of
interference from the Argentine leader General Juan
Manuel de Rosas.[44]

Despite its military failure Popham's intervention aided
British commercial ambitions. This had to be done by
maintaining a strict neutrality while insisting on full rights
of trade. The show of British naval power was often
coupled with diplomatic initiatives in Europe.[45] The
British extracted wartime concessions of trade in the Rio
de la Plata. Under these new conditions, British goods,
ships, traders and commission agents poured in during the
occupation, though they were rivalled by the Americans,
who in their vessels imported Africans, Cuban sugar, and
tobacco and exported hides, tallow, jerked beef and silver.

Such competition suited the British, for as long as they could trade on equal terms with others, and as long as neither the Spanish nor the insurgents interfered, they were satisfied. Only gradually did they come to view as necessary to their commercial purposes the independence of the colonists from Spain.[46]

At the same time as the British were attempting to stabilize the possibilities for profitable trade, the revolutionaries were making great gains. In 1810 and 1811 the revolutionaries overthrew the Spanish viceroys and captains general throughout Spanish America, and by the end of the war only Cuba and Puerto Rico remained. In Buenos Aires, in 1810, the Spanish captain-general was deposed and on 25 May, the day celebrated ever since as Argentina's independence day, a junta was established to govern in the name of the Spanish king but actually to rule independently. By their success, they avoided their predecessors' fate: embarkation on a vessel for lonely exile in the Malvinas.[47]

Argentina's progress in its early national period was marked by dissention between the capital and the pampas. Taxation and customs-house revenues also were subjects of internal dispute. At the same time Portugal and Brazil threatened the northeastern borders of the new state, which was actually a loose, uncertain confederacy dominated by the great river port. From this chaos came the federalist, then director, Juan Manuel de Rosas,[48] who dominated Buenos Aires and the confederation from 1829 to 1852, and who in his early years of rule brought an order of promise. It was the sort of regime the British regarded as propitious for profitable intercourse. In Argentina, as in other Latin American states, stability became the British goal, and men like Rosas agreeable and convenient if cautious allies.

Once independence of these states had been achieved, the British government put in place diplomatic representatives

whose duty was to foster advantageous commercial relations. The first diplomat sent to South America was the
envoy-extraordinary to the Portuguese Court in Brazil,
Lord Strangford, in 1808. Rio afforded an advantageous
location from which to communicate with the key cities
and provinces of Spanish–held South America. He pursued
several critical matters with the local government, including the suppression of the Portuguese-Brazilian slave
trade, and the attempted checking of Portuguese aggran-
dizement to the south of Brazil, especially in the Banda
Oriental, which Portugal invaded in 1811. Strangford did
not succeed in keeping Portugal out of the region.
However, he did keep Britain on friendly terms with the
revolutionaries whose triumphant years were not to be
seen until Argentina and Brazil were to wage a war and
Britain was to develop a diplomatic solution for the independence of Uruguay.[49]

Strangeford's successor was Lord John Ponsonby, in
1826 appointed envoy-extraordinary and minister plenipotentiary to Buenos Aires. Ponsonby believed that the
use of force would solve nothing in regards to British
policy in South America. His objective was to secure a
peace in the war between the Emperor of Brazil and the
government of Buenos Aires over Montevideo and the
Banda Oriental. 'Britain's interest in the Rio de la Plata was
unashamedly economic,' Professor Ferns concludes, and
Ponsonby's objectives, successfully achieved, was peace
for the purpose of British profit.[50]

In succession to Ponsonby, Sir Woodbine Parish, the
Hon. Henry Stephen Fox, and Sir William Gore Ouseley,
all served as British diplomats resident in South America,
and they feature in the diplomatic history of the Falkland
Islands or of Anglo–Argentine relations. All became experts
on South American affairs, and their opinions were treated
with respect by the ministers and secretaries at the Foreign
Office. They were the eyes and ears of the government in

Rio de Janeiro and Buenos Aires, and when circumstances warranted they could be exceedingly straightforward to the point of being blunt. In 1823, when the British government determined to send a representative to the Rio de la Plata, Parish was appointed commissioner and consul general. He was delivered to his post in H.M.S. *Cambridge*. First able to satisfy H.M.'s government on the subject of the stability of the Argentine government, he then concluded a treaty of amity and commerce with Buenos Aires on 2 February 1825. This was the first treaty made by any of the new states of the Americas, and the first *de jure* recognition of their national existence by any European power. Parish played a role, as we shall see, in bringing the question of the Falkland Islands to the attention of the British government.

Fox went out as the first British Minister Plenipotentiary to the Government of Buenos Aires in 1830.[51] His successor, Ouseley, went as secretary of the legation to Rio de Janeiro in 1832. In 1844 he was sent to Buenos Aires as British minister. Drawn into the problems of Uruguay, he secured the withdrawal of Argentine troops and their fleet from the capital Montevideo which, it must be added, was occupied briefly by British and French forces. He wrote about the region and his *Description of Views in South America, from Original Drawings made in Brazil*, the *River Plate, the Panama &c* was published in 1852. More abrasive than his predecessors, he did not endear himself to General Rosas and the Argentine government. He returned to England, devoted himself to anti-slavery measures, and put his energies into the chairmanship of the newly-founded Falkland Islands Company. [52]

While British governments were sending ministers and consuls such as Parish, Fox and Ouseley to the new South American governments they were also determined to make navigation safe in those seas. Surveys were the harbinger of commerce, the Hydrographic Office of the Admiralty argued, and given the rise of seaborne trade, the demand for accurate charts of dangerous shores, rivermouths and islands was acute. Hazards to navigation were frequent in unchartered waters. As 1825 mariners' sailing directions warned, captains who had doubled Cape Horn bound for the Rio de la Plata ought to give the eastern side of the Falklands 'a wide berth... on account of dangers supposed to lie about them.' Accordingly, in the same year, the Lords Commissioners of the Admiralty instructed Captain Phillip Parker King of H.M.S. *Adventure*, accompanied by the H.M.S. *Beagle*, commanded by Pringle Stokes, to survey the southern coasts of South America including the Falklands. King's instructions called for him to visit the territories newly-opened to British trade. On the basis of his observations he was to prepare charts and sailing instructions that would aid shipping and promote commerce. Subsequently, in 1831, Captain Robert FitzRoy commanded the *Beagle* on the second such South American survey, that in which the naturalist Charles Darwin made his own observations. FitzRoy's charts and sailing directions provided an important service to mariners rounding Cape Horn. FitzRoy also contributed an account of the value of the Falklands, Tierra del Fuego, and Patagonia. FitzRoy's achievements, made during years when no less than 250 British merchant vessels carried manufactured goods to South America, encouraged expansion of British interests, both political and commercial, in South America.[53] France and the United States showed similar interest by sending exploring expeditions in 1832 and 1838 respectively. In consequence of this work FitzRoy became the acknowledged authority on British navigation in the Rio de la Plata and Falkland Islands. FitzRoy never tired of promoting the wellbeing of the Falklands. Even then, he thought that Port Egmont was an ill-chosen base, that Port Louis or Puerto Soledad was too restrictive of access, and that another port – William or Stanley – would have to be selected for a seat of any projected colony.

On reflection, it may be seen that within the span of two decades of Popham's invasion of the Rio de la Plata, Great Britain's position as regards the affairs of South America had undergone its own revolution. The object of the policy of H.M.'s government was peace for the purpose of profit. That meant cordial relations wherever possible with the existing governments, reactionary, insurgent or otherwise. British policy towards Latin America had one over-riding aim: to secure the unimpeded, legal intercourse of British trade with colonies, ex-colonies or new states hitherto excluded by regulation. A new nation's independence did not guarantee British traders any special rights of access, and British diplomats had to work energetically to gain rights of trade on a fair and equitable basis. Nonetheless, 'by two main agencies – her trade and her fleet,' as the diplomatic historian Sir Charles Webster put it so succinctly, Britain was able to establish a very strong role in the affairs of Latin America, as indeed she was doing in almost every other continent in the nineteenth century. And in one other way was the Royal Navy a potent force: it prevented rival interference or an imperial reassertion by Spain. As the liberator Simon Bolivar exclaimed, 'only England, mistress of the seas, can protect us against the united force of European reaction.'[54]

In diplomatic channels of the world Britain was also underscoring the independence of the Latin American States. Britain did not want any French interference in Latin America, though she was not always successful in keeping her ancient rival at a distance from internal Latin American affairs. Thus the British Secretary of State for Foreign Affairs, Canning, made it abundantly clear to his French counterpart Polignac in 1823 'that the British Government absolutely disclaimed not only any desire of appropriating to itself any portion of the Spanish Colonies, but any intention of forming any connexion with them beyond those of amity and commercial intercourse.'[55]

If Canning secured French non-interference for the immediate future he also obtained an ally in American practice. The Americans were ever mindful of Britain's sovereignty of Canada and of Russia's possession of Alaska. They did not want to see any further aquisitions by these powers, and the Monroe Doctrine of the same year, 1823, made patently clear that they would not stand idly by and allow other states to make gains in their own back-yard.[56] That did not mean that the State Department would endeavour to gain all ex-colonial territories or annex all dominions of European powers in the western hemisphere. Indeed, after the Oregon arrangements of 1826 and 1827 Anglo-American relations entered a more relaxed phase than at any time since 1812. Moreover, given the small size of the United States Navy at this time there is much truth to the argument that Canning not only secured French non-interference for the present but he gave the protection of the British fleet to the Monroe Doctrine and effectively brought the United States into a leading role in any congresses on the future of Latin America. In all these ways, Britain built up a broadly-based network of influence in regards to the affairs of Argentina, Brazil and other governments of the hemisphere.[57]

Nonetheless, the Falkland Islands, an appendage of the continent, stood alone, largely separated from the world diplomacy of the 1820s which concerned itself so much with continental South America. That isolation did not long continue, and in due course the islands were again brought forward to preoccupy the minds of the governments, diplomats and naval officers of the three nations which formed 'the South Atlantic triangle' – Argentina, the United States and Great Britain.

# CHAPTER 3

# Britannia Triumphant, and the Argentine rival

At the close of the Napoleonic Wars, Great Britain possessed a string of bases advantageous to her position as Mistress of the Seas, for the strategic locations of these ports gave Britain a dominant position in every ocean save the Pacific.[1] 'Our policy,' said the Secretary of State, Viscount Castlereagh, in 1816, 'has been to secure the Empire against future attack. In order to do this we had acquired what in former days would have been thought romance – the keys of every great military position.'[2] In addition to Gibraltar, the Ionian Islands and Malta in the Mediterranean, Great Britain held Bermuda and Halifax in the North Atlantic, a host of islands in the West Indies, Ascension, Tristan de Cunha, St. Helena, and Simonstown, Cape Colony, in the South Atlantic, and Trincomalee, Mauritius and Bombay in the Indian Ocean. In short, her seaborne prowess rested not only on her commerce, her fleet and her sailors, but on these numerous anchors of empire in prime locations.[3]

The Cape of Good Hope had been regarded as so important to eastern trade and the securing of the communications with India as to be captured and kept from the Dutch and French at the close of the Napoleonic Wars. Besides the

Cape there were three others: St Helena, in British hands from 1651, when the East India Company secured it as a safe port against Dutch attack in those seas; Tristan da Cunha, a popular American ship's haven, annexed in 1816 so that France would not take it as a base from which to rescue the incarcerated Buonaparte; and Ascension, uninhabited until 1815 when the British garrisoned it upon Napoleon's arrival at St Helena seven hundred miles to the southeast, and dubbed 'the stone frigate' and run by a man-of-war's boats crew. These three were the volcanic islets of British empire in the South Atlantic.[4]

In time, the Falkland Islands came to assume an equally important position in British strategic thinking. This happened despite all attempts by government to reduce the size of the fleet to a peace-time strength, to cut naval estimates almost in half between 1815 and 1840, and to minimise commitments overseas wherever possible. The objects of British policy were to maintain national security and to create and preserve opportunities for British trade on a world-wide basis of fair and equitable terms.[5] Empire was not an end in itself. It was an often distasteful encumbridge necessary to national prosperity and security at home as on the distant seas and shores where British merchants or commission-agents sold the wares of Birmingham, London or Glasgow. Consequently, safeguarding the sealanes of British power and profit ranked as a preeminent necessity. Under these conditions the Falkland Islands assumed a regenerated position in the minds of British policy-makers.

More often than not in the imperial progression it was only when a rival threatened that Britain intervened. Britain's imperial objectives were determined, more often than not, by the state of international affairs. In regards to the Falkland Islands, as to any number of locations including such examples as New Zealand, British Columbia and western Australia, the imminent danger posed by foreign intervention induced Whitehall to act. Such policy-making was reactive in nature; the pre-emptive impulse lay at the root of so much British policy-making in this era and afterwards. Had the Argentine government not responded to American economic intrusions into what Argentine political leaders and statesmen regarded as their rightful domain both by the principles of international law and by actual measures of occupation it is doubtful if the British would have been so quick to add yet another island-cluster to their already numerous possessions overseas.

Argentina, or more precisely the United Provinces of the Rio de la Plata, with its seat of government at Buenos Aires, had declared formal independence from Spain on 9 July 1816. That independence having been attained, and a new government constituted, Argentina inherited, and so it has always argued, the ancient territorial possessions of the old viceroyalty from which it was founded, that is to say, the area of the South American continent between the Andes and the Atlantic, from the Rio de la Plata to Cape Horn, embracing Tierra del Fuego, the strait of Magellan, Staten and all other islands, including the Malvinas. Spanish captains-general at Buenos Aires had long exercised dominion over the Malvinas. When the viceroyalty of Buenos Aires had been established in 1775, the Malvinas lay within the region governed by the viceroy.[6] The Malvinas, so the Argentine government claimed as early as 1816, were part of the property and dominion of the new, sovereign republic.

Spain had kept a show of force at Puerto Soledad (Bougainville's old Port Louis on Berkeley Sound) at least until April 1811, when her struggle against revolutionaries from Patagonia to the Rio Grande forced their withdrawal to more pressing military assignments. At one time perhaps 150 personnel were stationed in these remote islands but eventually these persons all withdrew from Puerto Soledad. The Spanish left behind, so Lieutenant J. A. Moore of H.M. Brig *Rinaldo* discovered to his surprise some years later, about twenty wooden houses, all in good condition, and a small church. They also had abandoned wild cattle, horses, oxen and other livestock, and geese. As late as that date everything appeared in good order – even the bakehouse boasted all its utensils, as if the former occupants of Puerto Soledad intended to return.[7] Evidently the former residents had no fear of a British occupation, or, if you will, reoccupation.

For almost a decade beginning 1811 the Falklands had remained deserted. The French ship *Bordelais*, on a voyage to China in 1817, coasted near the Falklands and her commander M. Camille de Roquefeuil wrote rather laconically about the fact that France no longer had a seat of empire there. 'I wished that it would again occupy those islands, which, it is true, would not furnish any rich produce, but where many hands might be employed in their cultivation.' Then he warmed to its new prospects: 'This colony would be useful to our fisheries; it might serve also as a place of deportation, and would afford a vent to our superabundant population. Spain, which is on the point of being excluded from South America, could have no interest in preventing us: and even the power which embraces the world with its colonies and squadrons, could hardly look with a jealous eye on the occupation of this desolate coast.'[8] But as Camille de Roquefeuil knew, a resurgent France would not reclaim the Falklands. During this time, wrote Captain FitzRoy, with characteristic trenchancy, 'there was no problem upon those islands who claimed even a shadow of authority over them.'[9] On occasion, shipwrecked passengers and crew would fetch up on one of the lonely beaches. Succour and relief would sometimes, but not always, come from a sealer or whaler that happened to be cruising in the vicinity and able in the infrequently clear weather to sight warning fires of distress kept by the involuntary beachcombers. Sometimes an ungrateful shipwrecked crew, when rescued, would even abandon the rescuers on an uninhabited island.[10] One ship-master, Johathan Thorn of the *Tonquin*, attempted to maroon some of his personal enemies and would have succeeded in leaving them behind had not a gun been held to his head.[11] The islands were unlit, unchartered, unmarked. They were a graveyard of shipping. They claimed, among other victims, the French corvette *Uranie*, on a scientific expedition under Desaulses de Freycinet; on 14 February 1820 she was holed fatally on a submerged rock off Volunteer Point, at the entrance to Berkeley Sound. Apart from the casual visitors and wrecked ships crews, the Falklands were a no-man's land, ungarrisoned by Spain, abandoned by Britain, and claimed but as of yet unoccupied by the young and ambitious United Provinces of the Rio de la Plata.

All of this changed on 6 November 1820. On that date the commander of the Argentine frigate *Heroina*, mounting 30 guns, Colonel Daniel Jewitt, took formal 'possession', as he announced in his solemn proclamation, 'of these Islands, in the name of the Supreme Government of the United Provinces of South America.' The ceremony had been performed with all due ceremony. The blue and white Argentine national flag had been hoisted at the ruins of the fort, under salute of 21 guns from the frigate. This had been accomplished in the presence of several citizens of the United States and subjects of Great Britain.[12] The declaration of Argentine possession was read under their colours. The event, the Argentine Minister to the United States, Carlos Maria de Alvear, later advised the Secretary of State of the United States, the Hon. John Forsyth, constituted an act of 'formal and solemn possession'. It was, he said, one undertaken by the new government pursuant to Spain's evacuation of the islands 'in virtue of the triumphs obtained by the Argentines at sea, who entered as soon as possible and took possession of them.'[13]

The officer in charge of these proceedings, Don Daniel Jewitt, Colonel of the Argentine Marine, hailed from New

London, Connecticut. He had studied law, joined the United States Navy, and then went into privateering. Like many another naval officer of that era, Jewitt was a sailor of fortune.[14] Sometime after the War of 1812 he had entered Argentine service. [15] He had sailed from Buenos Aires on a variety of assignments and eight months later, in late October, he had reached Berkeley Sound, or as it was shown in Spanish charts, Bahia Anunciacion. His ship, an observer recalled a little uncritically, wore a very dilapidated appearance. Her crew was riddled with scurvy, and eighty out of a complement of 200 were sick or dead. Jewitt, it seems, had weathered a mutiny on board the frigate. However, trusting no one, he 'slept in his trousers, with a dirk belted round him, and a pair of pistols over his head.'[16] With as splendid urbanity Jewitt carried on, accepting the assistance of the British merchant captain James Weddell, Master R.N., to pilot him safely to anchor off the old, unoccupied village of Port Louis.

Weddell recorded the particulars of Jewitt's act of possession. He was somewhat taken aback by Jewitt's assumption of 'an air of power and authority beyond my expectation.' He found Jewitt extremely polite and much in need of help. Yet Weddell could see that unless he offered assitance Jewitt might well take matters into his own hands, use his forty soldiers fit to do duty, and even press Weddel's crew into Argentine service. '[I] therefore determined,' Weddell concluded in tones reminiscent of discretion being the better part of valour, 'to make him my friend by exchanging civilities.'[17]

The Argentine act of possession of Port Louis had been carried out formally, Weddell said. 'On this occasion,' his description noted,

the officers were all in full uniform, being that of our navy, which but ill accorded with the dilapidated state of the ship; but he [Jewitt] was wise enough to calculate the effect of such parade upon the minds of the masters of ships who were in the islands; and as he had laid claim to the wreck of the French ship [*Uranie*] to the entire exclusion of several vessels which had arrived, bound to New Shetland, he was aware that an authoritative appearance was necessary.

Jewitt's demeanour in exercising this, his first act of authority, struck terror into the minds of some of the ships-masters in that harbour. So afraid were they that they, too, would be plundered, robbed of all they had, and left defenseless in these southern spots of ocean and rock that one of them as a last resort brashly suggested taking up arms against Jewitt. Weddell was no fool. He counselled caution. He went one step farther and introduced the leading advocate of ruin to Jewitt, the consequence of which was that the affair subsided.[18]

Jewitt made crystal clear to Weddell the nature of his assignment. He advised that he intended to act 'with the most distinguished justice and politeness' to all friendly flags. He reported that 'a principal object' of his mission was 'to prevent the wanton destruction of the sources of supply to those whose necessities compel them to visit the islands, and to aid and assist such as require it to obtain a supply with least trouble and expense.'[19]

Indeed, there were just cause for the Argentine government to concern itself with conserving the sealing industry of the Falkland Islands. In fact, Argentina was the first conservation-minded authority to interest itself with the archipelago's future economy. Jewitt found as many as fifty foreign vessels, most of them sealers and whalers, in the islands. And for the information of his superiors, he listed some of the ships' names – the *Jane* from Leith, commanded by Weddell, the *Indian* of Liverpool, and the *Sprightly* of London, indeed six British vessels in all. American vessels were more numerous. From New York and Stonington, Connecticut, were ten vessels, including the *General Knox*, the *Free Gift*, and the *Hero*.[20] Jewitt gave notice to the masters of these vessels that the laws of Argentina forbade all fishing and hunting on the Malvinas, and he warned that offenders would be seized, charged and sent to Buenos Aires for trial. A sample notice reads as follows:

> State frigate *Heroina*, in Port Soledad, November 2, 1820. Sir, I have the honour of informing you that I have arrived in this port with a commission from the Supreme Government of the United Provinces of the Rio to la Plata to take possession of the islands on behalf of the country to which they belong by Natural Law. While carrying out this mission I want to do so with all the courtesy and respect for all friendly nations; one of the objectives of my mission is to prevent the destruction of resources necessary for all ships passing by and forced to cast anchor here, as well as to help them to obtain the necessary supplies, with minimum expenses and inconvenience. Since your presence here is not in competition with these purposes and in the belief that a personal meeting will be fruitful for both of us, I invite you to come aboard, where you'll be welcomed to stay for as long as you wish; I would also greatly appreciate your extending this invitation to any other British subject found in the vicinity; I am respectfully yours. Signed, Jewett, Colonel of the Navy of the United Provinces of South America and commander of the frigate *Heroina*.[21]

Clearly, the home government in Buenos Aires was keenly interested in economic development of the rich sea resources of Patagonia. They subsequently decreed that natives and inhabitants of that region could fish and trade without penalty. Foreigners permitted to settle and trade – provided they paid the corresponding fees for landing settlers effects – could also fish and trade but, again, provided they paid the appropriate duties.[22] Put differently, the Argentines were not excluding foreigners from trade. They were establishing economic regulation, admittedly with distasteful fees attached. In essence, the Malvinas were established as an Argentine exclusion zone to unauthorized foreign trade.

In 1823, three years after Jewitt sailed away on other assignments, Buenos Aires appointed a commandant of the Malvinas, one Don Pablo Areguati. In that same year, two entrepreneurs, Don Jorge Pacheco and Don Louis Vernet, obtained from the same government the exclusive use of the fishery, the cattle of East Malvinas, and tracts of land on the same island – a measure designed to give the enterprise a modicum of self-sufficiency. The brigs *Fenwick* and *Antelope*, bearing horses and supplies, and the armed schooner *Rafaela* destined for patrolling and regulating the sealing industry, set sail from Buenos Aires under the general command of Robert Schofield. The project proved distressing to the leader. 'The difficulties attendant on every new undertaking were in this instance so great,' Vernet later reported with sorrow, 'as to discourage the Director, Schofield, who abandoned it the following year, losing more than 30,000 dollars and ruining himself, so that dying shortly afterwards in Buenos Aires, he left his widow and small children in a state of indigence.'[23]

Avoiding a similar case of personal ruin now became the all-embracing goal of Don Louis Vernet. Of this amazing man we know all too little. Born in 1792, he seems to have been French by parentage, German by birth, South American by naturalization, and a former resident of Hamburg, the United States and Buenos Aires. He was, indeed, one of many cosmopolitan European-born merchant-promoters who became active in South American commerce. Regarded by visitors as a wellread man who could speak several languages, Vernet kept at Port Louis a good library of Spanish, German and English works. Lively conversation blessed his dinner table; his wife, Maria Saez de Vernet of Buenos Aires was a fine singer; and a grand piano graced a living room of their long, low, thick stone-walled, one storey house, the finest residence at Puerto Soledad. Fifteen slaves, some of them Indian convicts, kept up the Vernet establishment. The urbane character of the couple and the settlement pleased at least one visiting British naval officer, who had expected to find only rude shelters and rough sealers.[24] Though American diplomatic correspondence falsely portrayed Vernet as an uncultivated barbarian, a pirate and a scoundrel, he was, on the contrary, a person of considerable character. He possessed a dogged determination, had all the qualities of a born pioneer, especially resourcefulness, and he foresaw the fundamental value of the islands to maritime commerce in the southern oceans.[25] He was a true entrepreneur. His circular letters to mariners advertising the attractiveness of what had become virtually *his* islands afforded models of cautious reporting and accurate particulars as to existing supplies, stores, anchorages and known hazards.[26]

Vernet's enthusiasm to succeed knew no bounds. All his capabilities, energy, capital and connections he invested in his island empire. Sad to say, they yielded little but difficulty. Vernet faced a succession of heartbreaks. One by one his partners fell away. All three of the ships he purchased, and one of the five he chartered, were lost. Crops failed too. Yet each growing season found him making agricultural experiments but with little results. Progress came at a painful pace in all things: that which he expected to achieve in a year consumed five. His colonists would have had every good reason to be dismayed and disgruntled, and on at least one occasion they resolved to quit 'that ungrateful region,' as Vernet termed it.[27] If Vernet is forgiven a slight show of immodesty, the colonists did have a model of industry and dedication in he and his wife. The colonists kept to their assignments, held in affection to the Vernet and his wife by their unfailing image of their patience and constancy. What the slaves or even the exiles and convicts under Vernet's charge thought of such bonds of sentimental loyalty we do not know, but it is not difficult to imagine, escape being no easy prospect. But whether bonds of attachment were sentimental or otherwise, Vernet gradually turned Puerto Soledad into a paying proposition, and its reputation grew as a seabase of supply and repair in the South Atlantic. In one twelvemonth period alone his settlement produced eighty tons of salted fish, partly rock cod, which netted £1,600 in Brazil. Between 1826 and 1831 he settled about ninety persons in the Malvinas, and in 1828 he even issued paper money.[28]

Vernet was determined to develop the economic resources of the seas and shores of the islands. He held to the mercantilist views of his age. To his way of thinking, British ascendancy on the seas had been acquired by possession of that heavily-fought-for prize, Newfoundland, the British 'nursery of seamen'. In his memorandum of his occupation he revealed his understanding of the role played by the Newfoundland fishery in international affairs and particularly British maritime preeminence. 'Why should not the Fisheries and South become in the course of time proportionally as valuable to us as are those of the North to the English?' he asked. And how had England been able to profit from this? he queried. The answer, he said, was by excluding the rivals or by limiting their interests by treat. Argentina's future strength at sea must lie in the foundation of a national fishery 'which has been at all times, and in all countries, the origins and nursery of the Navy, and of the mercantile marine.'[29]

But the question was how to keep the islands and their

resources out of foreign hands. Vernet had found intruders in his island. Like Jewitt before him, he discovered that the foreign ships came to harvest all the sea resources they could – to seal and to catch whales. His twenty year monopoly, granted by Buenos Aires in 1823, counted for nothing with these interlopers.

Any decrees designed to give Proprietor Vernet sole control over the fisheries were really hollow unless backed up by a decent show of force. Vernet was the first to realize this, and he appealed to Buenos Aires authorities to send a strong frigate to cause the rights of the colony to be respected. They were unable to oblige. But by two decrees, both dated 10 June 1829, they invested Vernet with all the public and official character they could muster.

By the first, they established the Governorship of the Malvinas and Tierra del Fuego. When as a result of the glorious revolution of May 25, 1810, these provinces became independent from the Mother Country, Spain had effective possession of the Malvinas and all the other islands which surround Cape Horn, even the one which is known as Tierra del Fuego. This possession was justified by the right of first occupation, by the consent given by the main European maritime powers and by the proximity of these islands to the continent part of the Viceroyalty of Buenos Aires, entitled to govern them. For these reasons, and since the government of the republic has inherited all the rights the old Mother Country had over these Provinces, and which were exercised by the viceroys, it has continued to exert its authority on said islands, their ports and coastal areas. And even though it has not been possible to give to that part of the territory of the Republic the attention and care deserved, it is no longer possible to delay the adoption of measures to ensure the rights of the Republic enabling it to benefit from the production of said islands and to give the population the protection it deserves; the Government agrees and decrees:

a letter, dated 25 April, Parish gave a full report on what he understood to be transpiring in the Falklands. He reported there were 103 persons living there in Vernet's thriving colony. As to Vernet, he believed that his 'very intelligent person, apparently neglected by Buenos Aires, would be very pleased if His Majesty's Government took his settlement under their own protection.'[34] Even at that late hour, Parish did not know that Buenos Aires had under its own consideration the issuing of decrees that would enforce their claims to dominion and soon elevate Vernet to exalted rank. Thus Buenos Aires' decrees were promulgated before Parish's fierce warning of 25 April had reached the Foreign Office.

Besides Parish's distressed call for action, the British government was under pressure from three independent sources, all of them recommending reoccupation of the Falklands. First was that of a Mr. Beckington, promoter of western Australian settlement and of South Seas whaling. With all the florid capability of a true pamphleteer he wrote Sir Robert Peel, minister at the Home Office, to say that Britain could boast of having Heligoland, Gibraltar, Malta, the Cape of Good Hope, Bermuda and other prize spots which gave England command of the coasts or entrances to the Baltic, Mediterranean, Levant, Indian Ocean 'etc'. Now, he waxed eloquently, 'in the plentitude of power and in the hour of peace' the government should take possession of some port 'whose entrance if possible could effectually be defended against the intrusion of a moderately strong force, and might by degrees become the little Gibraltar of the South: either in the Falkland Islands, in the south part of the Continent, or even in Tierra del Fuego itself.' Peel was interested enough to send Beckington's letter on to the Colonial Office, which, in turn, passed it on to the Foreign Office for consideration.[35]

A second, more urgent, call for action came from the Commander-in-Chief on the South American Station,

Rear-Admiral Sir Robert Otway, who himself had received an anxious report from one of his captains, John Wilson of the frigate *Tribune*. Wilson had been in those seas, searching for privateers and pirates preying upon British merchantmen in the region of the Rio de la Plata. During his hunt, Wilson had put into Berkeley Sound. There he had chanced upon Venet's colony which now numbered fifty men, women and children and 1700 cattle. Wilson quickly came to the conclusion that such an active location ought to be British. 'Remember,' he advised the admiral, 'they are virtually ours, being ceded to us by Spain in full right of occupancy, though in the negotiations with that power, we acquiesed, if I remember rightly, in her reclaiming the sovereignty of them. The people of Buenos Ayres can have no pretensions whatever to them.'[36]

To this was added a third opinion, that of Lieutenant William Langdon, R.N. This officer shared the dubious distinction with countless others of his rank and station at that time: half-pay unemployment. After the Napoleonic wars he had turned his talents to profitable effect, and five times he had commanded merchant vessels to and from New South Wales, always returning to London by way of Cape Horn. From the perils of this seafaring he came to understand the requisite necessity of having a settlement in the Falklands for ships to go to for refit, provision and water – even as a refuge in case of accident. Ships masters, Langdon reasoned, would use the Horn route homeward bound with greater frequency if they could be assured of a port other than Montevideo or Rio, which lengthened their passage and incurred damaging charges. He thought the Falklands an ideal refuge. But again rivals loomed. Eighteen months previous he had put into Berkeley Sound. To his dismay he had found the islands taken possession of by a German overseer, Vernet, and about twenty men, mainly North Americans, who seemed to be making the islands a going concern for the investors, who were thought to be a company of merchant adventurers from Buenos Aires.[37] Langdon's member of parliament, Thomas Potter Macqueen, entreated on behalf of Langdon, and the whole served to bring credence to the view that while England slept a foreign rival was stealing the march on her. But the Colonial Office was advised of Langdon's warning, and this added grist to the mill. Not to be omitted is the fact that Langdon himself was not uninvolved in his own self-interested scheme, and took out with another Englishman, Whitington, his own grant of land in the Falklands, from none other than the Argentine governor, Vernet.

Thus one promoter might call for a 'little Gibraltar of the South,' another might propose a secure base for H.M. ships, and yet another might foster the idea of a British refuge for British merchantmen. But taken together these views added to points of view the ministry were obliged to consider. The combined weight of argument was in favour of extending British obligations.

The Colonial Office investigated the question of reoccupying the Falklands, and did so with a great deal of thoroughness. The report of the department on the subject noted that Sir George Murray, the Secretary of State for War and the Colonies, considered three points. The first of these was the pressures of merchants trading to South America and the Pacific, particularly as regards to the advantages of refit and refreshment, and as connected with the political questions of British expansion in that quarter. The second, more delicate matter was the surprising proceedings of the Argentine government in 'assuming to themselves the right to dispose of the Islands and the projects which they have in regard to them.' This was an intervention which obliged the Colonial Office to state categorically: 'it is clear from these communications that the time has now arrived when the claim of Great Britain must either be distinctly asserted or altogether abandoned.' The third point was whether the Falkland Islands might be used as a convict settlement and this at a time when the Australian colonies ought no longer to be considered as such. In short, there were three issues identified by the Colonial Office: maritime advantages, foreign threats, and convict settlement. The Colonial Office adopted the project of reoccupying the Falklands and advised other departments in a circular letter dated 22nd July 1829.[38]

To all of this, a determined resistance to any armed British reoccupation came from the Prime Minister, the sagacious Duke of Wellington. Uncertain of British claims and equally afraid of exciting the attention and jealousy of other powers, he stood squarely opposed to re-hoisting the Union Jack on the islands. 'It is not clear to me,' he wrote with suspicion on 25 July 1829, 'that we have ever possessed the sovereignty of all these islands....' Even if Britain's right to the Falkland Islands had been undisputed at the time of first occupation and indisputable now, he confessed that he would doubt the expediency of taking possession of them. 'We have possession of nearly every valuable post and colony in the world,' he added, 'and I confess that I am anxious to avoid exciting the attention and jealousy of other powers by extending our possessions and setting the example of the gratification of a desire to seize upon new territories....'[39]

But to sit and await foreign intervention could prove costly. He acknowledged and admitted the many costs of non-intervention:

> I am at the same time very sensible of the inconvenience which may be felt by this country, and of the injury which will be done to us if either the French or Americans should settle upon these islands, the former in virtue of any claim from former occupancy, the latter, or both, from any claim derived

by purchase or cession from the government of Buenos Aires. That which I would recommend is that the government of Buenos Aires should be very quietly, but very distinctly, informed that his Majesty has claims upon the Falkland Islands, and that his Majesty will not allow of any settlement upon, or any cession to individuals or foreign nations of these Islands by Buenos Aires, which shall be inconsistent with the King's acknowledged right of sovereignty. I think that this is all that can be done at present. It will have the effect of impeding any settlement or cession by Buenos Aires, and as we may suppose that the French and Americans will hear of this communication they will not be disposed to act in contravention to it unless determined upon a quarrel with this country.[40]

Wellington's view prevailed against the muted voice of anxiety raised by the First Lord of the Admiralty, Viscount Melville, who pressed upon cabinet the advantages and the necessary of a secure maritime base for British shipping in the southern seas.[41]

The Admiralty held the position that effective occupation constituted the only means of securing British claims of sovereignty. The Permanent Secretary of the Admiralty, Sir John Barrow, advising the Colonial Office on the necessity of a forward position, argued that the 'law of nations' dictated that 'priority of discovery must give way to priority of occupancy.'[42] Put differently, in Barrow's opinion, it was insufficient to claim territories by prescriptive right or even prior discovery; occupation must be made. Barrow's view had sound foundations in contemporary international law. By this time the law of nations recognized, according to William Blackstone and the widely-accepted Swiss international jurist Emerich de Vattel, that a nation could only have acknowledged sovereignty if it actually took possession and formed settlements or actually used the territory.[43]

These views were doubly strengthened by the Foreign Office's opinion that British rights had not lapsed through non-occupation and by the Colonial Secretary's belief that the time was right for a resumption of possession.[44] But Wellington barred the door. In reply to the earnest entreaties of his colleagues in cabinet he would not even consider re-occupying Port Egmont and placing there a garrison to protect the British claim. In his opinion Britain already had 30,000 troops stationed hither and yon around the world. No more obligations were needed. Besides, British interests in the distant Pacific were hardly sufficient to warrant further bases in or adjacent to that ocean.[45] Nor was he much concerned with the legalities of the matter, and he did not wait for the opinion of the King's Advocate (which actually advised that Britain's claims were still valid): the Falklands were not to be reoccupied and for the reasons given by the Iron Duke.[46]

In the circumstances, Aberdeen was thus really only able to thank Parish politely for the information contained in his anxious dispatches, and to advise that the Foreign Office could not yet sanction a reoccupation. In detail, he admitted that because of the rapid commercial and political development of South America the Falkland Islands had a great value for England as a naval base. In the event of Britain being engaged in a war in the Western Hemisphere such a station would be almost indispensible to the war's successful prosecution. Irrespective of these considerations, the time was not right for occupation: in his own guarded words, 'it is not in my power at this time to inform you of the final determination of His Majesty's Government with respect to these islands.' It was a question of 'much delicacy,' one demanding the 'most mature deliberation.' However, he instructed Parish (in whom he had the greatest confidence) to inform the Argentine government as forcefully as possible of 'the existence of His Majesty's pretensions.' He was to make clear that 'H.M. will not view with indifference nor can he recognize any cession of territory by the Government of Buenos Ayres either to individuals or to any foreign nation, which shall be found incompatible with the just rights of sovereignty to which H.M. lays claim, and which have hitherto been recognized by the Crown of Great Britain.'[47]

At this juncture, Britain's response to Argentina's occupation had to be confined to strongly-worded language. Aberdeen and Murray would have preferred something more forceful. Yet all that could be done, in the face of Wellington's resistance, on the Foreign Office's directive, was for Parish to deliver the note of protest to the Argentine Minister of Foreign Affairs, His Excellency General Tomas Guido. Guido received the British protestation and indicated that the government would give it particular consideration; he promised to communicate in reply once he had orders to do so.[48] Those orders never came. Buenos Aires never arrived at any resolution of the matter and never gave any official reply to the British note. General Rosas' government had a good many other matters to consider, not least civil war and a threat to its authority. Thus for a time the matter remained. Argentina disregarded the British protest and Britain took no action, that is, until the affair was brought again into prominence by Vernet's bold attempt to exercise his newly-acquired gubernational power and exclusive fishing rights.

In due course, Wellington and his administration passed from power, and in November 1830 the reform-minded cabinet of Earl Grey, Prime Minister and First Lord of the Treasury, took office. In key portfolios were three individuals who held strong views on maintaining national obligations, even at the risk of further overseas expansion: Viscount Palmerston as Foreign Secretary, Viscount

Goderich as Secretary for War and the Colonies, and Sir James Graham as First Lord of the Admiralty. Not to be forgotten were Lord John Russell, E.G. Stanley (later Lord Stanley and Earl of Derby), and Lord Auckland – all either in or near to the inner circle of this cabinet. As a group they stood clearly for the maintenance of national interests. As to the particular figures Palmerston, returning to that office, set the example as the epitome of the foreign secretary who demanded that British interests and rights be maintained in every quarter of the world. Similarly, Sir James Graham at the Admiralty was set on a complete administrative reorganization of the Navy coupled with cost-cutting measures. Thus, one could be assured that if the Falklands were again to be relegated to a secure place in the British Empire such a step would have to be 'done on the cheap'.

On the legal side the government now possessed a clear argument and opinion from the King's Advocate General that the British title was firm. 'I am humbly of opinion,' wrote Sir Herbert Jenner, King's Advocate General, on 28 July 1829 to the Earl of Aberdeen,

> that the right which this Country acquired by the original discovery and subsequent occupation of the Falklands Islands cannot be considered as in any manner affected by the transactions, which occurred previously to the year 1774. So far from those rights having been abandoned they have been always strenuously asserted and maintained, particularly in the memorable discussions with Spain referred to in your Lordship's letter, which terminated in the restoration of the English Settlement and Fort which had been taken by the Spanish Forces. The claim, therefore, to these Islands, now advanced by Buenos Ayres, cannot be admitted upon any supposed acknowledgement or recognition of the right of Spain

by this Country: if it is capable of being maintained on any ground, it must be upon the supposition, that the withdrawing of the British Troops in 1774, and the non-occupation of these Islands since that time, amounted to a virtual abandonment of the right originally acquired, and that, being unoccupied, the Islands in question reverted to their original state, and liable to become the property of the first person who might take possession of them. But I apprehend, that no such effect is to be attributed to either or both of these circumstances. The symbols of property and possession which were left upon the Islands sufficiently denote the Intention of the British Government to retain these rights which they had previously acquired over them, and to reassume the occupation of them when a convenient opportunity should occur.[49]

The King's Advocate General therefore concluded that upon these grounds the right acquired by the United Kingdom to the Falkland Islands had not been invalidated by anything which had occurred previous or subsequent to the year 1774. If the legal 'go-ahead had been supplied what was still wanting was the political will to do so. Such a will could not develop in a vacuum and perhaps could only be established under the stress of circumstances. British imperial policy was reactive in nature, more often than not meeting the needs of the day as they arose, or simply, 'muddling through'. Given the appropriate political will to effect an occupation the stage was now set for an intervention, a reassertion of right and claim to sovereignty by force and possession.

# CHAPTER 4
# The Eagle's Visitation

The Argentine decrees of 10 June 1829 brought forth two interventions: one American, one British. Of these, the first was swift and savage, the second was slow and overwhelming. The first reflected the United States' determination to have freedom of the seas for her fishermen, the second demonstrated Britain's will to secure a base valued by rivals. Argentina was on the receiving end of both these interventions, and reeled from the one only to be flattened by the other. Not that the United States and Great Britain planned this double blow. However, to bewildered Argentine ministers and diplomats it all must have seemed like a slick bit of collusion. How was it, they asked, that Washinton's rule for the Americas, the Monroe Doctrine forbidding on pain of retaliation a European nation's acquision of imperial territory in the Americas, had been conveniently allowed to lapse? And why, too, did the Americans, whose model republic offered such a noble example, exact such wicked vengeance on the new republic in its own moves of self-determination?

At the root of America's intervention in the Falkland Islands lay the United States' enshrinement of the principle of the Freedom of the Seas. To the United States and her sailors this policy was nothing short of a sacred trust. The nation had gone to war in 1812 to defend the principle, and had taught Great Britain that the ideal which the old mother country had herself proclaimed in earlier days was one which the Americans would also enforce with equal determination, at the mouths of their cannon if necessary.

Argentina's decrees and Vernet's exactions cut across the sanctified principle. More than this, they came directly into conflict with the burgeoning commercial interests of those American sealers and whalers who in the 1820s were scouring all the world's seas and shores in search of marine bounty. In any one year during that decade, twenty sealers and whalers wearing the Stars and Stripes would be found frequenting the waters and havens of the Falkland Islands. They came to hunt and to get provisions. And they thought little of, and cared less for, any exactions of Governor Vernet and his employees. One such vessel was the *Harriet*, an American schooner out of the Connecticut borough of Stonington and skippered by Gilbert R. Davison. This ship and this captain came to play a very lively role in the Falkland Islands saga. Other schooners and masters could have been 'named' by Vernet. However, the *Harriet* and Davison became the subjects of an international fury that had immediate ramifications in Argentine-American relations and long-standing legacies of distrust. And not without interest is the fact that they hailed from Stonington, a seaport of particular tough-minded folk who had fought off an attack by a British squadron in August 1814. Altogether it was not a place of faint-hearted souls, and it claimed to give the sealing trade its toughest men and its stoutest ships.

On 12 August 1830, Captain Davison had sailed in the *Harriet* from his home port on what he hoped would be a routine sealing voyage to the southern hemisphere. On 24 November he made the Falklands, where he put in for four days. Vernet met him, and Davison, who knew nothing of Argentina's newly-proclaimed dominion over the Malvinas, concluded that the German was *pretending* to act as governor of the islands and of the adjacent Chilean coast including the Strait of Magellan. Vernet warned Davison against taking any seals on property under his authority, and even gave him a printed paper setting forth his authority and containing a warning not to hunt seals. Davison steered for Cape Horn and Staten Island, took some skins, and was back again in the Falklands on 26 February 1830 where he remained for three or four months. At first Vernet proffered no resistance. But on 13 July a most surprised Davison was apprehended by Matthew Brisbane, Vernet's superintendent, flanked by a gang of armed men. He was advised that he would be going to see Vernet to answer to charges of sealing in and near Cape Horn. At first Davison refused but with Brisbane threatening violence he agreed to go to Port Louis. Once at the port he was put under lock and key. Armed sentries stood at the door. The *Harriet* was brought to the Argentine port of San Salvador, her papers were rummaged, her crew were confined, and her supplies were disembarked and sold. Fifty-four seal skins and seventy-eight hair-seal skins were laid out as testimony to breaches of Vernet's decrees. Two other vessels met a like fate: the *Breakwater*, Captain Carew, owned by the same Stonington interest, and the *Superior* Captain Stephen Congar, of New York. The three schooners were now tied at anchor side by side, the skippers were in prison, and the crews were being sent hither and yon – some to Rio de Janeiro, others to Buenos Aires, and still others, such as a seven-man boats crew of the *Superior*, were left on Staten Island to seal. The crew of the *Breakwater* made their own break for freedom. They took possession of the schooner, and left her skipper, poor Captain Carew, and four men stranded on the islands. They then sailed for the United States. For the moment American sealing in the Falklands faced ruin, and this splendid place which Yankee sealers and whalers had visited for upwards of fifty years was now proclaimed the sole property of a foreigner of uncertain credentials, or so the Americans reasoned.

Vernet, we know, had no armed ship at his disposal and no Agentine warship to hand. But he did have his governor's commission and his decrees and enough armed force to make patently clear to Davison and Congar that he intended to have his way. Vernet struck a deal with Davison: one vessel only would go to Buenos Aires as a prize for trial as a test case, the other would go sealing on the west coast of Chile, and that profits from the voyage would be divided or not divided if the Buenos Aires court condemned the one ship. Vernet and Davison then sailed in the *Harriet* for Buenos Aires on 7 November and arrived there on the 20th.

In Buenos Aires, Captain Davison immediately called on George Washington Slacum, the United States consul, and made a deposition detailing all the particulars of the outrage.[1] Slacum had represented to the Minister of Foreign Affairs, Thomas Manuel de Anchorena, that he was at a considerable loss to conceive 'upon what possible ground a bona-fide American vessel, while engaged in a lawful trade, should be captured by an officer of a friendly Government.' He added that he could not bring himself to believe that Buenos Aires would sanction an act which would disturb materially the cordial relations between the two countries. He asked the minister to lose no time in informing him if the Argentine government intended to 'avow and sustain the seizure.'[2] Anchorena explained in reply that there were bureaucratic delays while the ministry of war and marine made inquiries. Slacum's anger radiates from the pages of his next letter to Anchorena, dated 26 November. He reiterated his views and brashly suggested that the Minister deny in toto any right of Vernet to capture and detain American vessels engaged in fishing in the Falklands and in the islands and coasts about Cape Horn. And to cap it all Slacum stated that Anchorena ought to receive his letter as an official protest on behalf of the United States Government and against Argentina and all and every persons acting under its authority who had engaged in the illegal, forcible seizure in the Falkland Islands.[3]

Here, an American scholar has written, the bluntness and lack of consideration often displayed by American representatives came into evidence.[4] To Slacum's heated epistle, Anchorena replied in measured tones that he could not regard a consul's on-the-spot note as a formal protest of the United States government against Buenos Aires. All 'turbulent measures' should be shunned, Anchorena said, and he hoped that irrespective of whatever doubts would be raised by the United States government that the differences could be amicably resolved by a direct understanding between the two states.[5] By that measure Slacum found himself suspended from his post.

Ten days after Captain Davison of the *Harriet* made his deputation to Consul Slacum, the U.S. Sloop-of-War *Lexington* dropped anchor in Buenos Aires roads. Her captain, Silas Duncan, has been anchored off Montevideo, 120 miles distant, but on learning of the arrest of the *Harriet* he had proceeded with all possible speed to Buenos Aires. Captain Duncan was even more hot-tempered than Consul Slacum, and he stated that in view of the fact that American commercial and national interests were facing threats in the Falklands he intended to hasten there and protect American citizens and commerce. Under these new pressures Slacum twice represented to Anchorena a disavowal of Vernet's actions. And Duncan even wrote to Anchorena to give notice of his intended action in the *Lexington* unless he could get satisfaction. Then, in a clear representation of his own opinions of poor Vernet, gathered from his interviews with the Yankee skippers and crews, Duncan alleged to Anchorena that Vernet had plundered the *Harriet* of almost every article on board. He requested that Vernet be delivered up to the United States on charges of piracy and robbery, or that he be arrested and punished by Buenos Aires.[6] This was undiplomatic and uncalled for, and Anchorena who sensed an impending disaster soon took steps to defend his nation's interests both in regards to Vernet's seizure and the *Lexington*'s impending strike. Certainly, he did not reply hurriedly to Duncan's demand. Indeed, his rather feeble reply when it eventually came arrived too late. Consul Slacum later charged Anchorena with concocting a delayed reply so that the Argentine government should make it appear that Duncan's act was rash and intemperate. Sufficient time existing, Slacum charged, for Anchorena to have served whatever notice they wished without making it appear that the Americans intended something sinister.

In fact, Duncan went about his plans for a single-minded act of reprisal. Sailing from Buenos Aires roads, he brought the *Lexington* to anchor off Port Saint Louis on 28 December, with Captain Davison formerly of the *Harriet* on board as pilot. Witnesses declared that the *Lexington* entered Puerto Soledad under the French flag, and did not hoist American colours until before landing. But by virtue of this then common practice it is perhaps of small moment.[7] In regards to Duncan's further acts there can be no doubt that no forbearance was employed, no leniency spared in making this a rough reprisal. 'Truly,' as Maza, the Argentine Foreign Minister, was later to complain, 'Duncan spared no pains to make the outrage as humiliating and scandalous as possible.'[8] Duncan dispatched parties to shore. There they began their long litany of destruction. They set torches to buildings. They broke into houses. They ravaged gardens. They terrorised settlers. All of this brought Vernet's settlement to an end, and resulted in the loss of his tireless efforts.

Having destroyed the work of years, they now set about to ensure that it would not be reconstructed readily. They turned on its defences. They spiked the four guns at the Argentine fort. They threw rifles into the sea. They fired the magazine. Then the damage was extended to the boats. They confiscated an Argentine shallop, and they stove in every boat they could find. They seized all the seal skins that had previously been commandeered from the *Superior* and *Harriet*. In all, it was a quick and sudden blow, and without encountering any resistance Duncan was able to post a proclamation at the fort which stated that anyone who interfered with American fishing rights was a pirate.[9] Duncan also declared that effective 31 December the islands were free of all government.

In all of this the sole resistance to Duncan's actions had been that of Superintendent Matthew Brisbane, left in sole charge of Vernet in the latter's absence in Buenos Aires pending the outcome of the Davison-*Harriet* trial. Duncan considered him as in the same category as his superior – a rogue and pirate – and abused him rather badly on the quarterdeck of the *Lexington*. Then he was put in confinement. On Duncan's orders various persons in Vernet's employ were also arrested, held in confinement, and denied food. The *Lexington* sailed for Buenos Aires with Superintendent Brisbane and six Argentine men, all handcuffed day and night, and placed on the most meagre of rations.

Before sailing from the Falklands, Duncan took pains to gather depositions from various citizens. These sustained the view that Vernet's work, and that of his employees, was that of desperadoes and ruffians. He cited how American vessels were regarded as piratical, how American citizens were captured or stranded, and how Americans had to make new agreements with Vernet. His catalogue of grievances highlighted Vernet's usurpation, and once in Slacum's hands they were, with other reports, soon awaiting attention on the desk of the Secretary of State in Washington.[10]

News of this outrage had already reached the American capital by way of the schooner *Breakwater*, whose crew had challenged their skipper and broken from the grasp of Argentine guards. She had brought news to the United States government. The message was certainly garbled, and the precise details were quite uncertain. Yet the President, Andrew Jackson, himself a frontier fighter of no little repute and one well aware of British interests and aspirations in the Americas, had no doubts as to the authenticity of the *Breakwater's* report. 'In the course of the present year,' he said in his 6 December message to Congress, 'one of our vessels engaged in the pursuit of a trade which we have always enjoyed without molestation has been captured by a band acting, as they pretend, under the authority of the Government of Buenos Aires.' He had sent a warship to afford lawful protection to American commerce, and he intended sending a minister to inquire into the circumstances and the claims of the Argentine government.[11] Of course, he knew nothing of the intended proceedings of Duncan and the *Lexington* then at Buenos Aires preparing for her Falklands strike. The President and the Secretary of State were not at all in the dark about 'doings' in the Falklands. Indeed, in February 1831, nearly ten months before the *Lexington* action, the Secretary of State had sent advice to the chargé d'affaires at Buenos Aires warning of Vernet's demands on American sealers, requesting particulars of the legalities of Vernet's authority, and instructing him to remonstrate against Argentine acts. Long before the storm the United States had formulated its views on Argentine claims to sovereignty. In the words of the then Secretary of State, Martin Van Buren: 'The Government of Buenos Aires can certainly deduce no good title to these islands, to which those fisheries are appurtenant, from any fact connected with their history, in reference to the first discovery, occupancy, or exclusive possession of them by the subjects of Spain.'[12]

Once the *Breakwater's* news was reinforced by the additional material from Slacum and Duncan, the United States position hardened. Indeed, it did so with each successive snippet of information coming to Washington from the distant reaches of the South Atlantic. Three successive sets of instructions went out to Buenos Aires. These were dated 26 January, 14 February and 3 April 1832. The second of these contained a long catalogue of alleged Argentine crimes. This included imprisoning crews, leaving part of them on desert islands, sending others to distant parts, refusing them liberty to go to their vessel at the port of her condemnation, forcing others with service, and encouraging desertion. It also included reports of robbing ships and their cargoes and selling the same without trial or authority, and of robbing shipwrecked American mariners. These acts showed the Argentine persons as undertaking acts which merited United States' intervention and breaking up of the settlement as an act of necessary self-defence. And even if Argentina possessed title to the islands this did not allow them, Livingston said, 'to interfere with our right of fishing'.[13] The third set of instructions to Buenos Aires was sent subsequent to receipt of Captain Duncan's report on the incident, and it made crystal clear the President's entire approval of Duncan's conduct under the circumstances which he had detailed.[14] More than this, the American government advised its consul in Buenos Aires that he was to represent Duncan's actions as just. The Argentine government was to be advised that Duncan's acts were undertaken in protest to the seizing and trying of United States citizens as pirates and the annoying of American commerce. The consul was not to object to the removal of Argentine persons from the Falklands as this was done, so the Secretary of State reported, at their own request, and consequently it could not be considered an injury. Beyond this, the consul was to make it abundantly clear that Argentina had failed to give 'any orders to prevent the evil' when Slacum and Duncan had represented to the Argentine minister to avoid the threatened peril to the Falklands settlement.[15] The responsibility for the matter was to be put squarely on the head of the Argentine minister.

Francis Baylies was selected, it is said in his instructions, for his known discretion, industry and talent, and he had President Jackson's and Secretary of State Livingston's full authority to negotiate with the Buenos Aires government.[16] But the American statesman John Quincy Adams, with a touch of irony and maliciousness, considered him one of New England's 'most talented and worthless men.' It appears that he had been sent to Buenos Aires to appease him, for the President had deeply offended him by offering him the Collectorship of Customs at New Bedford. Inexperienced in diplomacy, highly charged in temperament, he was not the best of appointments. In any event, Baylies departed from Boston aboard the U.S.S. *Peacock* under orders of 26 January 1832 to get to his post as soon as possible. At the same time other vessels in the U.S. Navy were being sent to 'show the flag' and protect American fisheries from molestation by persons Washington was convinced were unauthorized by Buenos Aires and engaged in piratical acts.[17]

A little more than four months later Baylies had taken up his post. He immediately took the line that Slacum had kept to, though at first he was not as demonstrative or nearly as threatening. He denied the right of Argentina to prohibit fishing around the Falkland Islands. Of a new nature he demanded to know why American vessels had been discriminated against, since Vernet had not interfered with English ships, knowing full well that he dare not meddle with them. Baylies demanded full indemnity for American losses. He wanted Slacum's reinstatement. To the Argentine government he sent a long note in which he examined Argentine title to the islands (which he determined to be not defensible in international law) and a full report on the fisheries (which his government could not accede as within the terms of *mare clausum* that the Argentine government proported to be the case).[18]

In due course a reply came from Manual Vincente de Maza, acting Minister of Foreign Affairs. De Maza raised the matter of Slacum's suspension, and said that his government preferred dealing directly with Washington. On only one condition would the President, General Rosas, allow negotiations to continue: because the *Lexington's* raid was a barbaric crime Buenos Aires insisted on prompt and complete satisfaction for it. That meant reparation and indemnification to the government, to Vernet, and to the colonists for all damages and injuries.

Baylies was unyielding, and there the matter stood at an impasse. Offended and doubtless overly-zealous, he took the line that he must sever his connection with the government of Buenos Aires. He asked repeatedly for his passports, at last received them on 3 September, and sailed for the United States five days later. With him he took Slacum and all the archives of the United States legation. He anticipated that war would occur. Baylies's withdrawal bespoke frustration, and some observers thought it rather an intemperate and unnecessary act.[19] John Quincy Adams said, a little acidly, that Baylies had stayed in Buenos Aires just long enough to get the United States into 'a senseless and wicked quarrel' with Argentina. To this he had remarked: 'nothing but the imbecility of that South American abortion of a state saved him from indelible disgrace and this country from humiliation in that concern.'[20] Surely Baylies ought to have the last word on this himself. In reference to dealing with De Maza and the Argentines he wrote Secretary of State Livingston: 'We have attempted to soothe, and conciliate and coax these wayward petulant fools long enough.'[21]

The matter, however, never resulted in war. Baylies may

have been intemperate. De Maza may have been unyielding in insisting on discussing Duncan's raid before talking of Argentine fishing rights. But relations between the two countries were suspended for the moment though, as President Jackson appreciated, not broken off completely, for Washington awaited the arrival of the recently-appointed Argentine minister, General Carlos Marca de Alvear, who was expected to seek indemnification for the *Lexington* strike.[22]

Meanwhile in Buenos Aires, the British minister, the Hon. Henry Stephen Fox, was watching these proceedings with keen interest.[23] Of urbane charm and wit, Fox possessed tact and courteous manners which were to ease Britain's relations with Argentina at precisely the time that the United States was accerbating an already difficult position. Fox's despatches reported a constant turmoil in Argentine domestic affairs. Factions quarrelled in Buenos Airies while in the republic's distant provinces 'senseless, interminable, unintelligible discord' seemed the order of the day. There had been a furor in the local press about the *Lexington* business, and the government had taken every advantage, Fox told Lord Palmerston, the Foreign Secretary, to use the incident as a means of distraction from the internal discord which rocked the country. As to the incident, Fox reported to London that irritation and ill humour had been manifested on both the American and the Argentine side.[24]

As perplexing as the Argentine-American quarrel seemed to the British minister he knew that the South Atlantic triangle was heavily weighted on the side of cordial Anglo-American relations. He did not take immediate action on Palmerston's instructions to get the Argentine government to revoke Vernet's concession and governorship. Rather, he knew it was 'just as well to let the Americans do their own quarelling in Buenos Aires and that in any case an assertion of British sovereignty might very well involve Britain in disputes with the Americans about fishing rights.'[25] Fox could report with confidence to Palmerston that Baylies had told the Argentine government that the United States was prepared to acknowledge the sovereign rights of His Majesty. But by the same token, as the United States was a successor state of Great Britain in the Americas, the United States government claimed the same rights of fisheries as those of Great Britain – a well-argued view from the close of the American revolutionary war.[26] Fox's despatches did not indicate any unusual difficulty as far as the state of British interests was concerned: The Falklands had been left a wasteland without any visible authority, but for all of that he could not see an Anglo-Argentine war erupting.

Other information was reaching the government in London concerning these uncertainties, and most recommended British action. The British consul in Montevideo believed that the United States intended to 'question the dominion of the Falkland Islands with a view to establishing a right to fish therein.' A rumour circulated that American commercial interests were trying to buy out Vernet's partners or leaseholders. The British ambassador to Washington told Palmerston that the United States would not submit to Argentina's assumptions but at the same time they would not permit any interruption in the exercise of their lawful occasions in that part of the world. Rear-Admiral Sir Thomas Baker, the Commander-in-Chief, advised that at any time an American warship could be found stationed permanently in the Falkland Islands, and the sceptre of the U.S.S. *Essex* preying upon British merchant shipping in wartime was raised again. He issued orders to British warships on the South American station to 'narrowly watch' French ships of war who might use the American-Argentine difficulties as their long-awaited opportunity for a French occupation of the Falklands.[27] All these snippets of information and all of these recommendations for protecting British interests pointed to one fact: that Britain's Falklands policy was now bankrupt. Forbearance had been the order of the day while Argentine and American commercial interests had escalated to the point of a diplomatic rupture. Now that must change.

In London the initiative passed to the Admiralty, which had been receiving its own share of alarms from admirals and commanding officers on station and whose own views were already known to the more reluctant Foreign Office. More often than not the Foreign Office provided the initiative for imperial expansion based on information received from 'on-the-spot' authorities. Yet in the case of the Falklands it was the Admiralty which pressed the point. War was to be avoided, for the result of war would be more damaging to Britain than anything the nation could gain, advised Sir James Graham, the First Lord of the Admiralty.[28] However Palmerston did not intend any action that would lead to war. Besides, as he said in 1832, Great Britain stood at a high point in her foreign relations, more respected than ever before.[29] Other nations might threaten war with Britain; however, going to war was another matter, for against that superior power they would do so only at their peril. Provided the margin were clearly in Britain's favour, British ministers could do what they pleased, though they might come in for a certain amount of foreign rebuke.

The Admiralty – both Lord Commissioners and their secretaries – had maintained an ancient interest in the Falkland Islands, as we have seen. A recommendation to reoccupy had been their position in 1829. The Argentine-American fracas again brought their attention to a heightened position. Rear-Admiral Baker knew of Consul Slacum's threats, his demands for reparations and justice, and his calls for naval support. Baker's letter of 16 March 1832 reporting the *Lexington's* actions was read with gravity at a meeting of the Lords Commissioners of the

Admiralty in Whitehall on 7 May. That day the Board minuted tartly: 'Send copy to the Foreign Office and express their Lordships' anxiety to know whether the parties now in possession are under any existing treaties with Spain lawfully entitled to the Falkland Islands.'[30] Private discussions must have followed between cabinet ministers and perhaps their secretaries. On 4 August the Colonial Office learned of the Admiralty's intention to have one of H.M. ships passing Cape Horn call at Port Egmont, West Falkland, and assert British authority, and on 7 August the Admiralty sent the Foreign Office draft instructions for approval of the intended action.[31] Those orders called for the Commander-in-Chief on the South American station to exercise British rights of sovereignty, and (by a woefully modest measure) to maintain the right by dispatching an annual supply ship. At the same time, the British minister in Buenos Aires was to be advised of these proceedings.

To the initiative of the Admiralty, Lord Palmerston offered no resistance. Indeed, he may have solicited their Lordships' proposal. He approved the Admiralty's draft, and on the 30th of August wrote to the Secretary of the Admiralty 'signifying the King's pleasure' that a ship of war should proceed at once on the mission. In consequence, the necessary despatches were prepared by the Admiralty Secretary and the Foreign Office.[32] Foreign Office clerks now committed a clumsy error. They sent Minister Fox's correspondence on the impending measures to Rio de Janeiro rather than to Buenos Aires. By so doing they caught Fox's newly-arrived successor in Buenos Aires, Philip Yorke Gore, completely unawares. This apart, the proceedings were straightforward.[33] At last, British force to reoccupy the Falkland Islands was on its way.

# CHAPTER 5

# The Trident Strikes

Once taken, Whitehall's decision to reoccupy the Falkland Islands was put in the form of instructions and forwarded by dispatch to the Commander-in-Chief, South America, Rear-Admiral Sir Thomas Baker at Rio de Janeiro. Once received, Baker advised Captain J.J. Onslow of the *Clio* that the Lords Commissioners of the Admiralty in pursuance of the King's pleasure were to send a ship to Port Egmont in the Falklands 'for the purpose of exercising the rights of sovereignty there, and of acting at the said Islands as in a possession belonging to the crown of Great Britain.'[1] Onslow was instructed to put to sea the following morning, 29 November, and to proceed to Port Egmont 'with all expedition.' He was to make repairs at Port Egmont to the blockhouse and flag staff, and to keep the Union Jack constantly hoisted. He was to ascertain, by registration, the number, names, ages, nationalities and occupations of any persons he found there. If he met with no opposition he was on his return to Rio to give an account of proceedings to the Admiral, for the information of the Admiralty and H.M.'s Government.

Admiral Baker did not stop there, and he set down in precise detail the particulars as to what Onslow was to do if he were to meet with any hindrance. If he met with a foreign force he was first to acquaint the commander of it with the purpose of the mission, to request particulars as to why they were there in force in a British settlement, and to require, in civil terms, their flag (if hoisted) to be struck, and their force quickly withdrawn. 'You will then await his reply,' ran the orders, 'and, should he promptly comply with your request, you will, *under due caution*, afford every facility in your power for the embarkation and orderly departure of the foreign force in question, with any property to which such force may have a just claim.' Beyond this there were additional orders for certain particulars. If he were to meet with any resistance or objection he was 'providing you deem the force of the sloop under your command adequate to the duty of forcible expulsion' to command the commandant to order his troops to lay down their arms and 'quit forthwith at their peril the British possessions.' Even if this be complied with and resistance continued was Onslow to resort to force. Even then the caution was added that he was to use violence with only all possible moderation 'consistent with its effectual accomplishment.' He was not to allow any evasive delay or compromise if there were vessels there to take the military personnel away. His purpose was 'to keep up and maintain' the King's sovereign right. And, if he found the *Clio* of insufficient force, which Baker thought scarcely to be expected, Onslow was to give notice that they should withdraw, and if this were rejected he was to give them a solemn protest, in writing, of the consequences that would follow by their violation of the laws of nations 'and especially of the dignity and sacred rights of Great Britain.' Other than this he was to regard the armed occupants as 'illegal intruders.' If he could get no satisfaction he was to sail as soon as possible to Montevideo, where news of the circumstances could be got to His Majesty's minister at Buenos Aires, and if Baker himself were not in the Rio de la Plata he was to find out his position and rejoin his flag.[2]

Her Majesty's Sloop *Clio*, which bore the name of that seductive Muse of History, was a 389-ton sloop-of-war and carried a main armament of 18 thirty-two pounder guns. She was precisely the right instrument for such a task. She was a vessel in the Royal Navy of His Britannic Majesty, King William IV, 'the Sailor King'. If she were lacking in power and got into an unfortunate jam any number of men-of-war wearing the White Ensign were available for reinforcement, perhaps not immediately but in sufficient time that the weight of the British nation could be brought to bear on the affairs of any far-off coastal littoral or island cluster where national interests needed protection. Such was 'sloop-diplomacy'.

Ships such as H.M.S. *Clio* were a highly efficient means of influence in the age of sail. They were seen in all the world's great seas in the years after Waterloo. Whether they were securing British merchants from Barbary pirates or giving protection to nervous consuls, whether they were shipping antiquities from eastern states or freighting bullion from volatile places to the Bank of England – or indeed undertaking any number of duties attendant to Britain's predominant position in the world's affairs – men-of-war such as the *Clio* were the tools of empire. When coupled with adroit naval diplomacy as exercised by commanding officers, on carefully-worded instructions from superiors, that is, Commanders in-Chief, the Lords Commissioners of the Admiralty, and the Foreign Office, they could usually be ample enough means to bring the object to its conclusion. In the *Clio's* case that object was the reoccupation of the Falkland Islands.

The captain of the *Clio*, like the vessel under his command, was the epitome of his breed. Commander John James Onslow, Royal Navy, age 37, derived from an ancient Shropshire family whose fighting experience dated from keeping the Welsh on the borders in check. One of his ancestors had been a distinguished Speaker of the

House of Commons, and young Onslow could boast of his share of connections or 'interest' so essential for advancement. His father, Admiral Sir Richard Onslow, Bart., G.C.B., Lieutenant-General of Marines, or 'Old Dick' as he was more commonly and affectionately known in the Service, seems to have been as tough a fighter as could be found during the naval wars of the late eighteenth century which reached their climax at Trafalgar.[3] His mother, Anne, also had the Navy in her blood, her father being Commodore Matthew Mitchell. John James, their second son, had entered the Navy in 1810 as a volunteer first-class, that is, he was destined to become an officer. Subsequently he had served on the coast of Spain, in the South Atlantic and on the South American and on the Jamaican stations. Promoted to lieutenant on 5 September 1816 and to Commander on 23 April 1822, he enjoyed a wide range of South American experience, and during the protracted period of peace after 1815 which kept so many commissioned officers 'on the beach' on half pay, John James was rather regularly employed.[4] Onslow had been on half pay since 1826, and had secured the post of Inspector Commander of the Coast Guard at Great Yarmouth. That meant that from his office-residence at Telegraph House, Marine Parade, he had responsibility for keeping in check the artful smugglers of that coast. In character, like his father, he was a no-nonsense type yet not quite so irritable or excitable.

John James Onslow had been appointed to the command of the *Clio* then fitting out for the South American station, on 30 April 1830. He could expect that not only would he have an interesting assignment, particularly in view of the revolutionary and nationalist enthusiasm then sweeping South American states and provinces, but that he might very well come home a wealthy man, for the *Clio*'s duties would more likely than not extend to the Pacific Ocean. This would allow him to take on a shipment of specie at

West Coast ports as far north as Mexico for freighting to Rio and home in the *Clio* at the completion of a three-or-four-year commission. The course of this tour of duty would see the vessel, as was customary in that age of far-flung 'showing the flag', visiting Valparaiso, Callao, Guayaquil and Panama, the islands of the South Seas, and the Mexican coast so rich in silver, so prone to anarchy where the presence of the White Ensign afforded salutary security to merchants, British and other.[5] As it turned out, Onslow gained no financial remuneration from the Falklands episode. But when he returned to Portsmouth from Rio de Janeiro at the end of his commission on 3 June 1833 he had a freight of no less than 880,000 Mexican dollars (worth perhaps 17,600 pounds sterling) in the hold of the *Clio*, of which he was entitled by regulation to one-half of one percent, an equal portion being split between the station admiral and the Greenwich Hospital for Seamen.[6]

Though Onslow and the *Clio* were given the specifically designated duty of reasserting his Majesty's claims to the Falkland Islands, the Commander-in-Chief on the South American Station had calculated on the side of strength against any foreseeable margin of error. How embarrassing it might have been had the Argentine forces been superior to those of the *Clio*. To make certain that there could be no mistake, no Argentine successful resistance that would oblige an even more powerful British expedition to act so far away from secure and safe lines of communication and supply, Rear-Admiral Baker had H.M.S. *Tyne*, mounting 28 guns, and commanded by Captain Charles Hope.[7] look-in at the Falklands at about the same time as the *Clio*. The *Tyne* was destined for the Pacific, and to deliver, as her first duty, Mr. Bedford Hinton Wilson, His Majesty's Consul General to the Government of Peru, to his destination.[8] And though it must have appeared likely that Argentine forces would offer but little resistance, in the event the tenacious position of the defenders left no doubt as to the wisdom of Rear-Admiral Baker's precaution to send sufficient force.[9]

The instructions which Commander Onslow possessed carried the full weight of the British government and the knowledge and support of the king. These orders had been carefully arrived at after extensive discussion among interested government departments, their ministers, and their senior departmental heads. They were not issued with any degree of excitement but rather in a cool, matter-of-fact manner, for in that age instructions primarily from the Foreign Office, usually with clearance supplied from the Colonial Office and War Office and almost invariably the support or knowledge of the Treasury, were routinely being sent to consuls, ambassadors, Royal Engineers, and admirals and naval officers in every quarter of the world where British interests required succour. Those to Commander Onslow had their origin with the Admiralty and carried the blessing of the Secretary of State for Foreign Affairs, Viscount Palmerston. They were dated 28 November 1832 at Rio de Janeiro on board the flagship, H.M.S. *Warspite*. They advised Onslow that the Lords Commissioners of the Admiralty in pursuance of his Majesty's pleasure had decided to send a ship to Port Egmont 'for the purpose of excercising the rights of sovereignty there, and of acting at the said Islands as in a possession belonging to the crown of Great Britain.'[10]

The *Clio* sailed from Rio to the Falklands on 29 November, in close company with the frigate *Tyne*, Captain Hope. The voyage consumed little more than three weeks. During this time the *Clio's* gun crews, marines, and parties of small-arms men were drilled. Onslow had carronades, or 'smashers,' brought up from storage and placed in position. Approaching the Falkland Islands he read the articles of war. The *Clio* was ready for action.

On 20 December the *Clio* came to anchor in Port Egmont, off the ruins of Ford George on Saunders Island.[11] The place was deserted. He could find no squatters. All it was necessary for Commander Onslow to do to indicate British ownership was post a notice ashore saying that he had been there to exercise the right of sovereignty. He left at the fort this inscription: 'Visited by H.B.M. *Clio*, for the purpose of exercising the right of sovereignty over these Islands, 23rd December 1832.' It was a message of simple fact but hardly enough in itself to ward off any would-be attackers.

From the quiet desolation of Port Egmont where a Union Jack kept watch on foreign intrusion the *Clio* sailed to the energetic settlement of Puerto Luis de Soledad, the scene of so many hopes and so many dreams: of Bougainville's settlement, of Spain's garrison, of Jewitt's Argentine colony, of Vernet's profitable entrepôt, now of Argentina's new presidio.

Some months after Silas Duncan's savage stroke, Argentina had decided to secure her sovereignty by keeping a regular garrison at Puerto Soledad. In all, it was a small establishment, consisting of a sergeant's guard of soldiers, officered by a subaltern and a field officer. This new formal display by Argentine men-at-arms had experienced a troublesome beginning. The Commanding Officer was an absolute bear for drill and order, unceasingly parading his charges to the neglect of his men's dietary needs. The soldiers had no time to obtain sufficient food for good health, and lived on far worse fare than the settlers. The men of the guard considered the regimen unnecessarily severe, and after renewed warnings and threats they staged a revolt and murdered the Commanding Officer. For a brief interval the mutineers held away at Puerto Soledad. The armed schooner *Sarandí* arrived from Buenos Aires in October 1832, and the force on board, helped by some sailors at hand, put down the revolt. Now Argentina's dominion was kept by an altogether different crew under an altogether different regimen: now it was an armed camp, and the place resembled a presidio.

The *Clio*'s arrival at Puerto Soledad caught the Argentines by surprise. Onslow brought the *Clio* to anchor in the afternoon of 2 January 1833. The weather was moderate, with rain and cloud. The settlement lay peacefully under the Buenos Aires flag. Riding at anchor was the *Sarandí*, under command of Don José Marca Pinedo, Colonel of the Marine. At 38 years of age and one year older than Onslow, Pinedo was a distinguished and seasoned artillery officer and sea captain. Pinedo had been sent from Buenos Aires to keep watch on the restive soldiers of the garrison who had rioted and caused a good deal of damage to persons and property. The colony was under the authority of the new governor, His Excellency Juan Esteban Mestivier, who only recently had put down the revolt that had included among other barbarities the killing of his predecessor as governor.[12] However, Pinedo was in authority on land and afloat as he told Onslow, and there were twenty-five fine soldiers at the ready. The place was an armed camp, a devil's island where ex-mainland convicts lived in uneasy proximity to Vernet's settlers. Here the good order which Pinedo and Mestivier were working to re-establish was now disturbed by the British armed presence.

Once the *Clio* was moored Onslow went to see Pinedo. Onslow's 'courtesy was flawless,' historian Boyson has written of the encounter, but 'it was also winter-cold.' Onslow recorded the proceedings. 'I acquainted him civilly with the object of my mission,' Onslow recalled of his meeting with Pinedo, 'and requested him to embark his forces and haul down his flag on shore, he being in a possession belonging to the crown of Great Britain.' The Argentine account differs. It states that Pinedo sent two officers to the *Clio* 'to make the corresponding offers of attention and friendship.' But they returned to the *Sarandí* with news that Onslow intended to go on board the Argentine schooner at a later time.[13] This he did at 3 p.m.

Onslow states that in response to his request that Pinedo withdraw, the latter at first acquiesced, provided that Onslow agree to put the matter in writing, which he did. The Argentine view is that Pinedo protested against the British threat. He considered it a 'gross outrage' committed by 'a friendly and powerful nation which has always boasted of its fidelity and moderation, and has lost no opportunity of manifesting the cordiality of its feelings towards the Argentine republic.' Onslow held his ground. He said that duty required him not to consent to Argentine's pretensions unless ordered to do so by his government. His instructions, he explained, were to take possession, and he intended to do so the following day – hopefully at a time when the Argentines had struck their own flag. On this, Onslow took his leave. Onslow now sent his promised note.[14] It indicated his intention to hoist the Union Jack the following morning, 'when on request you will be pleased to haul down your flag on shore, and withdraw your forces, taking with you all stores, etc. belonging to your government.' To this Pinedo decided to send a deputation to the *Clio* to parley with Onslow, to repeat the protests, and to tell him that if he was going to use force that Pinedo would be obliged to reply in kind. The Argentines hoped to persuade Onslow to refer the matter to London. They did not succeed. Onslow refused a further meeting. The matter was closed. All the de deputation could do was return to the *Sarandí*, which they did at 10 p.m.

Early the next morning, the third, Commandant Pinedo went on board the British vessel to make one last protest against the act the British intended to commit. The Argentine view is that Pinedo agreed to withdraw but asked for more time – until Saturday the fifth, when he would sail with all the force besides all settlers who expressed a desire to quit the place. Onslow did not waver. He considered Pinedo's request inadmissible; and he told Pinedo that he must consider that he was in a British port. He also told Pinedo that he could not defer the execution of his orders, that Pinedo could see what force the British had, and there was more, that is the *Tyne*, on the way. In short, Onslow told Pinedo defiantly that he could therefore act as he thought fit. Pinedo issued one last defiant and proud declaration: Britain was responsible for 'the insult, and the violation of the dignity of the Republic and of its rights, which were thus inconsistently and disrespectfully trampled on by force.' He said he would withdraw. On no condition, however, would he pull down his nation's flag.

Onslow's view is that Pinedo now 'wavered' and was 'reluctant' to haul down the Argentine colours. This led Onslow to order three boats lowered from the *Clio*, and at nine o'clock marines and seamen landed at the point of Port Saint Louis. They placed a flagstaff at the house of an Englishman, about 'four squares' distance from the Commandant's residence. They then hoisted the Union Jack, Next they struck the flag of the Argentine Republic, and delivered it to an officer who was sent from the *Sarandí* to receive it for the Commandant. Pinedo was ready to withdraw from the scene of the 'insult.' But two days passed before the weather allowed him to make sail in safety, and to carry his complaint to Buenos Aires. The *Sarandí* put to sea. During the voyage home, Onslow wrote, 'the soldiers mutinied, and shot their commander; and from all I could learn from the commander of the schooner, great insubordination existed in this settlement, which paralyzed the settlers; and had we not arrived might have led to worse consequences, as there were a great many bad characters who left in the national schooner.'[15]

Thus without a shot being fired did the British secure peaceful possession of Puerto Soledad and restore by occupation their ancient if neglected claims to the Falkland Islands. Onslow's manner was brisque and uncompromising, and was not of the usual firm-but-friendly type meeted out by colonial administrators. He was on a specific naval mission; he had his instructions. Distance from home allowed for no communications, no referal, no second thoughts.

The *Clio* arrived in Montevideo roadstead on 19 January, a few days after *Sarandí* brought the news from Puerto Soledad. Onslow immediately sent a detailed letter of proceedings to Rear-Admiral Baker and an even longer report to the British chargé d'affaires in Buenos Aires.[16] His mission accomplished, he now proceeded to Rio de Janeiro. The *Clio* was back in Portsmouth on 3 June 1833, where she was soon paid off. As for Onslow, his days of excitement in foreign duties came to an abrupt end. He was put on half pay and reached the post-rank of Captain on 27 August 1834. He managed to get one more command – the corvette *Daphne* – and went to the Pacific in 1842–47. He spent the rest of his days in forced idleness at his Blofield, Norfolk home, where he died in 1856, aged 60.[17]

The official Argentine account of the *Clio* visit differed materially from Onslow's. Pinedo's dispatch reached Buenos Aires' outer roads on 15 January. Pinedo, contrary to British report, was still very much alive: indeed, curious to relate, he lived long enough for his government to punish him for not fighting to defend their claims. At once, on receiving details, two government ministers, Balcarge and De Maza, drew up a lengthy memorandum for the Argentine House of Assembly detailing the ousting of their flag and countrymen from the Malvinas.[18] Their report charged Onslow with dishonouring the Argentine flag. Onslow's act, they stated, violated the territorial integrity of the republic, its rights of justice, and its expectations of friendly treatment by the British government. In short, Onslow's act constituted a 'new and scandalous agression.' It was one more remarkable than that committed by Duncan and the U.S.S. *Lexington* the year before, for Britain and Argentine had enjoyed reciprocal relations and treaties of friendship and commerce. The incident exhibited 'a most flagrant abuse of power.' Argentina intended to defend its rights, to seek reparation from the British government, and to obtain 'the acknowledgement of our right to the Malvinas, and the exercise of our dominion over that territory.' If this could not be achieved, then Argentina intended to cry foul and to declare to the world that she was abused by a government which had wished to be considered 'as ranking amongst the most free and enlightened of Europe.' And to this declaration Britain would not be able to remain indifferent, or so the Argentine government reasoned.

In the strongest of terms Manuel Vincente de Maza, the Minister of Grace and Justice, informed the British chargé d'affaires, Philip Yorke Gore, that his government found the *Clio's* 'doings' unjustifiable. Public feelings had been greatly aroused. What had led to this, he asked? What had been undertaken which had so openly compromised Argentina's dignity and her rights to the Malvinas? De Maza asked for 'competent explanations'.

Gore's reply was polite and abrupt: he had received no instructions from London to make any communication with Buenos Aires on this subject. He would refer it to H.M.'s Government. He concluded with courteous assurances of his high and distinguished consideration.'[19]

De Maza was not satisfied with this curt reply. The next day found the two men face to face exchanging views, with neither giving quarter. De Maza complained that his government had been put in position of great embarrassment: British action was inreconciliable with the harmonious relations hitherto enjoyed by the two countries. Argentina was affronted: in respect to what had taken place, De Maza argued, his government could not but see a gratuitous excuse of the sight of the Strongest' to humiliate and depress a powerless and an infant people.' Had negotiations broken down his government could understand. As

it had happened the act had to be regarded as one 'infring-
ing on her Rights, and derogatory to her Dignity as an
independent Nation.' To those views Gore had only one
reply: surely the reoccupation could be no matter of surprise, for the 1829 warning had made the position of
H.M.'s government abundantly clear.[20] There the diplomatic difficulties remained until particulars of the transac-
tion reached the Argentine minister in London who took
the initiative in dealing with Lord Palmerston.

In London on 24 April 1833, Moreno represented to
Palmerston that his government requested to be informed
whether in fact the British government had given orders to
pull down the Argentine flag, and to take possession of the
islands in the name of the British sovereign.[21] The tone of
Moreno's message was sombre, its tenor indicating a hope
that the matter had all been an unhappy, unnecessary
mistake. Palmerston's unrepentant reply was that the
proceedings of the Commander of the *Clio* took place
in consequence of instructions given His Majesty's
government to Rear-Admiral Baker, the Commander-
in-Chief of the South American station; 'that this commander had orders to send a ship-of-war to the Malvinas
Islands, there to exercise the undoubted rights of
sovereignty which are vested in His Majesty, and to act in
that quarter as in a possession belonging to the crown of
Great Britain, and, of course, in case of meeting in those
islands any foreign persons on military force not
acknowledging the authority of His Majesty, the commander of the ship-of-war was to request such persons
and such military force to withdraw, and he was to assist
them with the means to do so.'[22]

This drew from M. Moreno a very long and elaborate
protest in which he maintained that any title on account
of prior discovery was doubtful. And as regards occupa-
tioĥ, British withdrawal signified the end of British
sovereignty.[23]

Lord Palamerston gave this question serious consideration and did not treat the matter cavalierly as the delay of
six months in getting a reply to Moreno tends to indicate.
The Foreign Office again solicited the views of the King's
Advocate-General, whose opinion of 30 November
became the basis for Palmerston's sharp reply. The King's
Advocate advised Palmerston to steer away from any discussion as to the first occupation or possession of the Falklands, because that would only lead to 'a protracted
correspondence, which would probably not end in any
satisfactory result.' Thus as regards Moreno's protest
Palmerston held that he would not admit 'either the
accuracy of the statement, or the soundness of the argument.' Palmerston reminded Moreno that Consul Parish's
protest of 19 November 1829 against Argentine decrees
and land grants had gone unheeded by Buenos Aires. That
protest had made known, first, that Argentine authority
over the Falklands was incompatible with the British
sovereign rights, second, that those rights as founded on
discovery and occupation had been recognized by Spain in
1771, third, that Britain's 1774 withdrawal did not invali-
date Britain's just rights because that withdrawal took
place only in consequence of retrenchment, and, fourth,
that marks and signals of possession and property were left
behind to indicate ownership and an intention to resume
the occupation at a later date. 'The government of the
United Provinces of the Rio de la Plata,' Palmerston continued with cold directness, 'could not have expected, after
the explicit declaration which had been so formally made
of the right of the crown of Great Britain to the islands in
question, that his Majesty would silently submit to such a
course of proceedings: nor could that government have
been surprised at the step which His Majesty thought
proper to take, in order to the resumption of rights which
had never been abandoned, and which had only been permitted to lie dormant, under circumstances which had

been explained to the Buenos Ayrean government.'[24] And as to any 'secret promise' between Spain and Great Britain which would have kept alive some continuity of claim by Argentina, a thorough search of British archives had unearthed no such document. Palmerston could thus conclude that there was no evidence to suggest any such undertaking between British and Spanish governments. In fact, the documents he did produce pointed clearly to Spain's full acceptance of Britain's claims.

Nonetheless, Argentina persisted in pressing their case. Moreno brought the question forward again, on 29 December. Seven years later, in 1841, he addressed Lord Aberdeen, the Secretary of State for Foreign Affairs, on precisely the same points. But Aberdeen, like Palmerston before him, kept to the same line: that the agreement between Spain and Britain held, and any change to it by Britain was unthinkable. Thus the past was clear. As to the present and future the British position was equally clear: Britain would not permit any infraction of her incontestable rights. One last, passionate protest came from Moreno on 8 March 1842, but the Foreign Office with petulant authority advised that the question was closed.[25]

Meanwhile, in Argentina the *Clio*'s action at Puerto Soledad had inflamed the Buenos Aires public. General Rosas' party took every opportunity to foster anti-foreign feeling, the intention being, the resident British minister reported, to deflect some of the periodic disturbances away from the government. This necessitated a more regular watch by British warships in the Rio de la Plata, and almost invariably a sloop-of-war stood in Buenos Aires roads. This may have been some comfort to anxious British merchants and residents who had to suffer several indignities, not least inflamatory placards posted all over the city reading such things as DEATH TO ALL ENGLISH, and calling upon the citizens "to expel all British subjects from the Argentine dominions."[26] The

British minister's reports to the Foreign Office seldom failed to note the irritated and hostile feeling of the Argentines towards the British government.

Nonetheless, the British government had secured its prize. Altogether this little piece of imperial expansion had generated heat but not war. The United Stated had been agreeably comfortable with the British diplomatic stand. Even the return of the Union Jack to the South Atlantic did not strike Washington as in any way a violation of the Monroe Doctrine. The costs to British goodwill among the sovereign nations of South America was slight, at least from the more narrowly British point of view. Bolivia was the only country to rally to the Argentine position and declare the British act as a "grievous offence" that was offensive and extremely injurious to all the American republics."[27] But Bolivia made no representation to the British government, and other South American nations kept similarly silent. In London, worries of South American alienation did not enter the heads of British ministers or department secretaries. To them the issue was a legal one, pure and simple. British rights to the sovereignty of the Falkland Islands were indisputable. However, if they were certain about British *rights*, they were uncertain about British *occupation*. And in the subsequent decade they were to demonstrate that they had formulated no plan for the Falklands and were obliged to 'meet the needs of the day as they arose' in the pursuit of a colonial policy. They had reasserted sovereignty to keep out their rivals. In doing so they had not given the least degree of forethought as to what would be done with the Falkland Islands in the future. That fact alone makes the destruction and removal of Vernet's thriving colony a travesty of human progress.

# CHAPTER 6
# John Bull's Isles

With that wonderful degree of assuredness and optimism perhaps commensurate with the security provided by the splendid confines of their Board Room in Whitehall the Lords Commissioners of the Admiralty intended that the British presence in the Falklands should and indeed could be maintained by the annual call of one single warship. Such a casual display of authority could hardly control the continuing anarchy. Violence, murder and bloodshed became the order of the day in lieu of a permanent force to maintain law and order. Only by experience did the British learn the painful lesson: that civil unrest in the islands would oblige them to make provision for a regular government, and one that would cost the British taxpayer more dearly than anyone could ever have expected.

When H.M.S. *Clio* had sailed from Puerto Soledad leaving the Union Jack flying in the breeze she had left behind a ramshackle colony. The U.S.S. *Lexington* had done most of the damage a year before, but Captain Onslow had shipped on board the *Clio* all the Argentine supplies of Vernet's heroic rebuilding scheme of the intervening time. The few employees of the hapless and broken Vernet and the handful of persons who could not find their way to more comfortable, more genial locations were left behind – to live and to quarrel, to murder or to die.

Thus when Captain Onslow departed, the islands were blessed with even less government than when he had arrived. In these unhappy circumstances, the few survivors of the derelict colony were left at the mercy of the ex-convicts, ex-garrison soldiers, and exiled gauchos who formed the human population. A very good if sombre and sinister portrait of this community was given by the clear-thinking Robert FitzRoy, Commander in the Royal Navy, who on 1 March 1833 brought the surveying brig H.M.S. *Beagle* to anchor off the settlement.[1] He went ashore to find out why the settlement looked so dishevelled and why the Buenos Aires flag was not flying, as it had been during his visit two years before. He learned from Matthew Brisbane, Vernet's superintendent and agent, that the *Lexington*, in Brisbane's words, had 'ruined it.' The settlers had scattered to the country, afraid of any men-of-war. Occasionally sealing and whaling crews visited Berkeley Sound doing damage to property. The gauchos oozed disaffection and wanted to return to the mainland. A number of Spanish-speaking persons were there, twenty in number by one count, and there were three women, two of whom were negresses.[2] There seem to have been eight native South American convicts in Vernet's employ and, of a completely different sort, a few hardy, God-fearing colonists. In the latter category, besides Brisbane, there was the Irishman William Dickson. He was a dolt, to Fitz-Roy's way of thinking, and to his careless hands Captain Onslow foolishly had entrusted the task of keeping the Union Jack flying, and of raising it and lowering it (in agitated fashion) whenever a vessel should enter port. Onslow had shared FitzRoy's assessment of Dickson's mental capacities, but confessed that given the paucity of Britons present on the island he had no alternative in view.[3] Another settler of questionable brilliance, one Mr. Henry Chaffers, ran the store. Among the more progressive beings was Captain William Low, reputedly an ex-pirate but now a sealing-sailor and entrepreneur, who was working desperately hard to advance the maritime well-being of the colony and to assume the role of ship provisioner, one left vacant by the departure of Vernet.[4]

In all, the Falklands residents of 1833 formed a rag tag group, brought together by the most curious chain of circumstances. They were ungoverned and unprotected. FitzRoy recognized this anarchy, while Charles Darwin, as of yet largely innocent of man's inhumanity to man, marvelled at how Englishmen found their way to every corner of the globe.[5] At least the place was quiet, Darwin said, though he added with a touch of sadness: 'In the time of the old Spaniards, when it was a Botany Bay for Buenos Aires, it was in a much more flourishing condition.' FitzRoy's duties were in surveying, not in fostering British colonial settlements, and on 6 April the *Beagle* sailed from the Falklands for work on the coast of South America. Once more the islands were unguarded. 'Of this miserable seat of discord,' Darwin wrote on the same day to his sister, 'here, we, in dog-in-a-manger fashion seize an island and leave to protect it a Union Jack.'[6]

For a few months after the departure of the *Beagle*, isolation and quietness reigned in the islands. Occasionally a vessel put in for supplies. Otherwise the colonist-providers and the gauchos went about their business.

Then, all of a sudden a reign of terror occurred and with it mass murder. No one knows precisely what caused the rising. Settler Whitington says Vernet's eight Indian convicts rose against the settlers. The raw details are as follows. On 26 August a party of people were murdered, including Brisbane, Dickson, Don Ventura, Pasos Antonio Vehingar (or Anton Wagnar), and the captanz of the gauchos, Juan Simon. They were all the principal persons of the settlement. Captain Low, away on a sealing expedition, escaped death. Others, consisted of thirteen men, three women and two children, had fled to Hog Island, at

the head of Berkeley Sound, where they lived on birds
eggs until saved by the British whaler *Hopeful*. Lieutenant
Henry Rea, R.N., a scientific officer assigned to the merchant ship *Hopeful* by the Admiralty to investigate high
southern latitudes, found the settlement ravaged and ran-
sacked. He had run up the British flag, and sent a sharp
note of warning:

> As it is uncertain to whose hand this may fall, I have
> not entered into many particulars that have come to
> my knowledge; but I feel convinced, that if an
> English ship of war does not arrive here soon, more
> murders will take place....[7]

Rae possessed no authority to take any action to secure
British interests there, but he hoped the Commander-in-
Chief, South America, a British consul or the Admiralty
would take appropriate measures.[8]

Gradually the pieces of the crime were put together.
Five Indian convicts – Manuel Gonzales, Lucian Flores,
Manuel Godoy, Felipe Salazar, and one Lattore – had
joined with three gauchos – the leader Antonio Rivero
(pictured in English sources as desperado, described in
Argentine sources as a patriot in rebellion), José Marca
Luna, and Juan Barsido. Armed with whatever weapons
they had been able to lay their hands on – muskets, pistols,
swords, dirks and knives – they had gone to Brisbane's
house and killed him. It was cold-blooded, premeditated
murder. Then had followed a terrible trail of massacre.
One by one all of the victims had been hunted down. The
lucky survivors, who suffered a night of terror, had fled to
the fragile security of Hog Island in the harbour. The
assailants had grabbed what they wanted, had loaded their
horses with booty, and had headed for whatever hiding
they could find in the hills. Thus did the eight murderers
come into undisputed possession of East Falkland.[9]

Meanwhile, the Lords Commissioners of the Admiralty came under added pressure to establish authority in the Falklands. The captains of the *Clio*, *Tyne* and *Beagle* had sent reports warning of anarchy. Captain Onslow had recommended a small force to preserve authority and protect settlers. Captain Hope of the *Tyne* had urged the planting of a British settlement.[10] And the British consul general designate to Peru, Bedford Hinton Wilson, when at the Falklands in the *Tyne*, in early 1833 had come enthusiastically to the conclusion that a lieutenant and guard would suffice.[11] Eventually, on 14 August 1833, the Admiralty took up Onslow's and Wilson's plan and the assignment went to the First Lieutenant of the *Tyne*, Henry Smith, of whom more presently. With him were to be four seamen, as a boat's crew for his use and protection. The seamen were to be volunteers, for obvious reasons. They went from Portsmouth to Rio and hence to their new dominion of rock and water via the first available ship, H.M.S. *Challenger*, 28 guns, Captain Michael Seymour. The *Challenger* reached Rio at a time when Lieutenant Rea's distress call was already at hand. Accordingly, the Commander-in-Chief dispatched Captain Seymour on his business as soon as was conveniently possible. She arrived in Berkeley Sound on 7 January 1834 just in time to secure the imperilled colonists huddled on Hog Island from further threat.

On 10 January Lieutenant Henry Smith took up the esteemed post as the first British Resident on East Falklands. He constituted the first representative of British authority in the Falkland Islands since Lieutenant Clayton had abandonned Port Egmont, West Falkland (under reasons of economy) sixty years before, in 1774. Smith had risen in the Navy since his entry as a Volunteer First Class in 1810, and he had accumulated a successful war service and a steady post-war employment record. But given the government economies of the day, half-pay had loomed

large for poor Henry, as it did for so many other lieu-
tenants. Captain Hope of the *Tyne*, in which ship Smith
had been First Lieutenant, thought he would serve well in
the Falklands. Accordingly, Smith had been sent there.
Whether it was his desire to plant a British colony in the
southern hemisphere or, more likely, a desire to avoid
inactivity at home, he was classified as a volunteer for this
service. His four-man boats' crew was the same. Smith's
status was that of Resident, or, at the most exalted,
Lieutenant-Governor, though visitors like Darwin
thought him merely an acting governor. Technically
speaking, he was carried on the Admiralty's account as a
Supernumerary Lieutenant of the Flag Ship in South
America. In other words, he was governor of a 'stone
frigate,' answerable to the Commander-in-Chief, South
America, headquartered in Rio. He carried full authority
from his superior and specific instructions 'to keep the Flag
flying.' His allowance was seven shillings per diem in
addition to his full pay as supernumerary lieutenant (the
Admiralty's way of saying he was on half-pay), including
all allowances for rations. This was a handsome enough
hardship allowance, one might surmise, and a good means
of accumulating capital for private purposes, including
advancing loans to local residents. The seaman with him
were likewise given an isolation benefit, but of a much
smaller scale of two shillings per man per day.[12]

To give weight to the Resident's arrival and position, on
10 January 1834 at noon precisely, Smith had the Union
Jack hoisted. The *Challenger* provided a salute of twenty-one
guns. All around the flagstaff lay a scene of desolation. The
settlement was in total shambles. The best house available
was selected for repair as the Resident's House, and on the
11th the *Challenger's* carpenter with a gang of men began
repairs to the residence of the king's representative in the
South Atlantic.

Further news of the massacre greeted Smith on his

arrival. Accompanied by a marine guard temporarily left him by the captain of the *Challenger* he immediately went about the tasks of policeman-detective. On horse and foot, over rocks and through streams, he and his men combed the eastern islands. They did so without initial success. The *Challenger* went about other duties, though the marines stayed for this special assignment and, in due course, a second hunt was mounted – this time a successful one – and Antonio Rivero and his band, who had been at large in the Falklands wilds for seven months, were at last hunted down and seized. They were brought back to Port Louis on 7 March, and put in irons.[13]

Like most Falklands episodes this one also had a curious ending: the accused were subsequently conveyed to London with witnesses in the *Snake* for trial and thence to London's Newgate prison. But the judge dismissed the case for want of evidence, and in consequence they found themselves back in Rio. The Commander-in-Chief, Rear-Admiral Sir Graham Eden Hamond, became furious at this turn of events, for the accused had been sent back to him without any indication as to what he was to do with them. 'It is a very slovenly way of doing business,' he confided to his diary, 'thus throwing the onus of letting these rascals escape upon my shoulders, if I choose to let them go.'[14] But he did, and they were released in Montevideo.

Such a strange and unsatisfactory episode gave Rear-Admiral Hamond pause to consider the merits of the Falklands and certainly the legal difficulties of Britain maintaining them as a possession. Hamond was as conscientious a flag officer as could be found in the Service, and he had grown acutely anxious as to the state of British interests in the Falklands. In December 1834 he decided to go there himself, in the flagship *Spartiate*, 76 guns. But the ship met some very heavy, midsummer weather, and Hamond decided that the object was not sufficiently important to risk disabling the vessel, and he was obliged to return to Rio.[15] He had to content himself with sending other vessels, including the brig *Rapid*, commanded by Lieutenant Frederic Patten, and with ordering other warships such as were bound round the Horn or destined home from the Pacific to put into Berkeley Sound to support the flag.[16]

Left largely to his own devices, thrown back on his own resources, Lieutenant Smith set about the fearful task of making the colony self-sufficient. He reared vegetables, especially potatoes and turnips, and he cultivated corn. He kept records of climate and weather. He gathered notes about soil, local productions, facilities for naval establishments, and commercial possibilities. In all these things he did remarkably well, and his crops were so bountiful that scurvy-stricken crews of whalers were restored to health by his welcome produce. He also tamed cattle and horses. He raised poultry and hogs. Like the enterprising Vernet before him, he became guardian of his island-empire's resources, even issuing edicts to foreign vessels that they must desist from fishing or sealing round or near the islands. Failing this, they would be proceeded against as trespassers.[17] As to the habitations and other structures, he set himself, in the apt words of one of the settlers, 'to repair any damage inflicted by the vindictiveness and even inhumanity of American and English sealing masters, who . . . seemed actually to take a pleasure in destroying the sources from which other navigators might thereafter obtain similar relief.'[18]

Smith was a born pioneer and despite all difficulties, by the time he had completed his assignment he had just cause to write to the Lords Commissioners of the Admiralty indicating his personal contribution to the well-being of British empire in those seas. The ironic, even sardonic tone of his letter would not have been lost on his superiors. 'The nature of my position when first landed here was the total absence of medical assistance and the great dependence upon my own resources, pecuniary as well as otherwise, for most of the necessaries of life for the men under my control as well as for myself.' At the end of his rule, 350 tame cattle were on hand for slaughter, 850 hides had been sold (to the Crown's profit of 4,200 Spanish dollars), the gardens had been cultivated at his own expense, and a great volume of supplies and seeds were on hand. When he had arrived in 1834 he had for support four seamen and no gunboat. Now the Admiralty had deemed it necessary to replace him with 'a Lieutenant, a Vessel of War mounting 10 guns and 44 men (including a medical man) and artificers supplied with seeds and implements of all kinds.'[19] Not least, they were providing the requisite funds to carry on the work he himself had undertaken at his own expense and credit. He was rightfully aggrieved. At least, however, he had avoided half-pay status, something he had previously experienced. And he went on to have a successful career: he was promoted to Commander in 1841 and to Captain in 1846 and was employed on particular service in the steam-vessel *Rattler*.[20]

Smith was perhaps the kindest British friend the Falklands ever had. He never tired of advising the commander-in-chief, as he did first to Rear-Admiral Seymour on 18 July 1834 and subsequently to Rear-Admiral Hamond, that the islands could afford a useful place of refreshment for ships doubling and redoubling Cape Horn. Secure in British hands these islands would be beneficial to further British discoveries. They would also offer great prospects in whaling. However, they must be settled, Smith urged, and this could best be done by hardy fishing folk from islands north of Scotland. In regards to matters of strategy, the Falklands were unquestionably valuable, Smith noted, for '....should it ever be the fate of England to be at war with the whole continent of America, here is the key to the Pacific as well as a nursery for making a hardy race of sailors.'[21]

Yet British authority on the islands remained extremely fragile, maintained only by a skeleton force of armed personnel. Smith had charge of what amounted to a volunteer band of armed gauchos, brought from Montevideo and other South American ports in British men-of-war, and who with their families maintained the frail British presence. They kept garrisons at East and West Falklands. They manned lookout points in the principal western islands. They were on guard against American whalers whose masters and crews acted in piratical ways, chiefly stealing live-stock. From time to time they were strengthened by British warships that would arrive on missions of inspection and inquiry, their commanders carrying instructions as surrogate judges to try and punish offenders in a way similar to the ancient administration of justice in Newfoundland. This authority was also under constant pressure from certain citizens of Buenos Aires or Montevideo who wanted to settle on the islands. The commander-in-chief classified these persons as 'unauthorized.' Periodically he even referred to them in his correspondence with London as 'pirates' and 'brigands,' and refused to sanction their settlement until a British government was formed there on a permanent basis.[22]

While Smith coped and Hamond worried, London faltered. In 1835 a new ministry was formed, the third in ten months; and in this period of rotating-door cabinets, matters for Admiralty consideration did not receive rapid attention. The Falklands' status was Hamond's most nagging problem. Yet he could get no directive from the Admiralty as to whether or not a regular government and colony were to be established, or if the place was to be abandoned altogether. Between Lord Grey's 1832-4 ministry and Lord Melbourne's 1835 cabinet a good deal of mischief was nearly done as to Britain's Falklands policy, and the views of cabinet members reveal no high regard for the importance of the Falklands. Yet Palmerston was back at the Foreign Office in 1835, and he put a stop to a scheme mounted by T. Spring Rice and Lord Glenelg, successively Secretaries of State for War and the Colonies, to withdraw Resident Smith and to revert to an earlier regimen of securing British interests by casual calls of warships. The point was, Palmerston cautioned the well-intentioned Glenelg, 'whether in the present state of our discussion with Buenos Aires respecting the Sovereignty of the Falkland Islands, the entire withdrawal of the occupying detachment might not wear the appearance of an abandonment of our claims.' Glenelg had no counter to this fundamentally precise argument. In consequence, he did an about-face and agreed with his colleague. He ordered dispatches to be sent to the Admiralty advising Their Lordships to keep Smith's force at strength in order to 'prevent the settlement of foreign intruders,' to guard the wild cattle against destruction, and to preserve the Falkland Islands for the Crown.[23]

In addition, the Foreign Office came into possession of some valuable data from the minister in Rio de Janeiro, William Gore Ouseley. His long and rambling despatches to Lord Palmerston described the Falklands as an under-valued possession of the Crown. Capable of great economic production and a future depôt for steamers and sailing ships, they were useless owing to the nature of the naval administration there. He also believed a free port in those seas would stop the exorbitant exactions that the South American governments placed on foreign shipping in their ports. The Falklands might have the same relations to South American as Formosa did to China. Such a port, a headquarters of trade and of ship repair and shipbuilding, would assist the steady ascendancy of British seaborne activities along the coasts of South America.[24] Such views appealed to the security-conscious Palmerston, who wavered in no way from the position he had first adopted in 1832.

If the Ministry had cleared the air about the necessity of keeping the Falklands in order to deter any Argentine claims or occupation they were now beset with the unavoidable question as to the utility of the Falklands themselves. A very thorough and useful report had come from the senior naval officer in the Pacific, Commodore Francis Mason, C.B., who called in the islands in 1834. His view was that the British had no option but to stay, and that the islands had substantial commercial value. Even if colonization were not contemplated, he asked

> might not the rights of sovereignty be maintained, and the Islands offered in grants to those who choose to settle threat; for the dog in the manger renders the islands useless and unavailable to everyone. As things stand at present it is doubtful to whom the country belongs. England long since has claimed it and has armed herself to assert that claim, the Spanish government disputed the right and does still hold itself the lawful proprietor; and the Buenos Ayrean Government, highly indignant at the British assumption, claim the whole as naturally appertaining to their Republic. It is true the English flag is now flying here, and an Officer established as Resident remains there with four seamen attached to him; but this party is at times (by being necessarily detached) so completely in the power of the Buenos Ayrean [and] other strangers settled here, so inefficient to the protection of the cattle and other property, and so inadequate to curb the insolence and rapacity of the whalers and other rabble that occasionally congregate here, that it is in reality unsafe for the parties themselves, and by no means creditable to the country that its flag should be displayed over a territory where there is no power to maintain its respectability. . . .[25]

As to their geopolitical value in relation to South America and the Pacific, Commodore Mason was likewise level-headed. To his way of thinking there were only two questions: would it be advantageous in time of peace to commerce to have a base in the Falklands, and would it be advantageous in time of war to command the trade of the South Seas and to overawe the Agentine Republic in the event of armed conflict with that state? And to Mason these questions had obvious answers in the affirmative.

The task of evaluating the economic value of the Falklands fell to Captain the Hon. George Grey of H.M.S. *Cleopatra*, who in 1837 conducted an extensive, ten-week long examination. In his report, Grey evaluated the Falklands in the best way he knew how: in relative merits to Northumberland and the Borders – Grey country! The fourth son of the second Earl Grey, this twenty-seven year old post captain thought Smith's house looked 'like some preventive station on the coast of Northumberland.' He was delighted with the cattle, hogs, and poultry. The butter and milk were excellent, as good as any he had ever tasted at the ancestral seat, Howick. The steep shores, bare hills, intersecting ravines, tireless landscape and low-hanging clouds brought to mind bright images of the Cheviot Hills or the Scotch Moor on a winter's day. Alas, the mid-summer temperatures did not approach those of home, but it was warm enough at $63^0$F. What Grey seems not to have reported on was whether the salmon, if they existed, would rise to the fly.

Such sentimental diary data did not find itself of the desk of the Secretary of the Admiralty, but Grey demonstrated that in addition to his sensitive imagery (always by comparison to his beloved Howick) he was an astute judge of a place's strategic value, and this sort of argument counted in Whitehall. The Falklands, Grey advised his superiors, would form a useful station as regard British communication with the Pacific, for the islands offered abundant, secure harbours for merchant vessels to await a fair wind for rounding Cape Horn. In his estimation, the islands could offer a profitable settlement for such persons who could be established there. Water was readily available, and spars could be obtained from Patagonia. But, once again, to keep it secure and prevent it from becoming the haunt of pirates or privateers, a well-manned garrison of marines was needed.[26] Though Lieutenant Smith was there keeping the flag with a number of sailors, gaucho volunteers and their families, this constituted far from an adequate protection of British interests.[27]

As Captain Grey warned, pressures against British control in the late 1830s were coming from American whalers and sealers continuing to frequent the islands. Their crews would scramble ashore and kill wild cattle for hides.[28] Substantiated reports of these depredations led Rear-Admiral Hamond in 1837 to send another vessel, H.M.S. *Sparrow*, to the Falklands to report on the state of British interests. Her commander was to press for the recognition of British possession of the islands in the face of growing foreign commercial pressure.[29] The *Sparrow*'s commander warned interlopers such as the French whaler *La Perseverance* that the British government had the right to prevent foreign vessels from fishing within three miles of the shore 'which belongs to it *de jure* and which it occupies *de facto*.'[30] His orders allowed him to exclude fishing interlopers for a year and to arrest cattle and wild animal hunters. Hamond, however, complained to the Admiralty that he did not possess precise instructions that would allow him to protect by force if necessary the territorial limits of the Falklands, more particularly from the fishing interests of the Buenos Aireans, whom he said, were supported by the United States.[31] British naval officers who visited the Falklands would report finding signs of rival traders using the islands. In one instance, an officer found that the Americans kept an aged vessel at anchor at

Ship Harbour, New Island, as a depôt for ships of an American merchant named Barrow which were employed in the Islands, Cape Horn, and Patagonia. Oil barrels and spars lay on the beach nearby, and there were other signs that foreign sealers were frequenting the islands. In response to Hamond's request, the Admiralty and the Foreign Office proceeded to examine the correctness and propriety of extending British jurisdiction in the inshore or territorial waters of the Falklands. The Queen's Advocate-Geneeral, John Dodson, thought the Admiralty's draft instructions to Hamond 'correct and proper,' and thus when the instructions were sent Hamond was empowered to order the ships and men under his command to warn off foreign vessels fishing within the territorial limits of the Falkland Islands.[32]

Because of foreign activities in the islands, the commander-in-chief, on advice of the Foreign Office, had strict instructions to send periodically one of the ships on the station to visit the Falklands and to report on foreigners who went there to fish and seal.[33] Officers on these assignments carried orders to report on the state of wild cattle, to advise on the possibilities of cultivating vegetables, and to warn of any encroachments or settlements by foreigners. They were instructed to patch up injured ships and send them home for repair. On occasion British warships would transport agricultural supplies and livestock to the islands in renewed attempts to make the colonists self-sufficient.[34] The principal duty of such ships was to protect national interests, and to keep a close watch on the activities of foreigners, not least American vessels which, as one officer complained in 1841, 'did an infinity of mischief upon the islands.'[35] In actuality, the effectiveness of the Royal Navy in this watchdog role was only as good as the resources placed at the disposal of the commander-in-chief, and from time to time, as did Rear-Admiral Hamond in 1836, that officer would complain grievously of the meagre size of his squadron. Under strained circumstances of a Latin America in seeming disarray and constant anarchy, no ship-of-war could be stationed permanently in the Falklands where pressing matters made a visible presence of the white ensign a constant necessity for the preservation of British interests.[36]

In these circumstances, the Lords of the Admiralty were not unmindful of the needs of protecting British interests in the Falklands but it was altogether a matter of finance and departmental responsibility. Under Foreign Office advice to keep a sharp eye out for alien depredations, a decision was made by Their Lordships to despatch, from Portsmouth, a naval lieutenant attached loosely to the South American station (and dependent on it for stores and supplies) in a small vessel. This officer would be sea-lord of the islands. The first of these was Lieutenant Robert Lowcay. He took up his station in the ketch *Arrow*, carrying to the islands, sheep, fowl and seed.[37] Poor Lowcay failed to win much respect from his Commander-in-Chief, Rear-Admiral Hamond, on account of his undiplomatic conduct, his failure to inform his superior of vital information respecting rival French ship movements, and his poor sailing abilities. Lowcay made a cursory reconnaissance of the islands, and despite his superior's misgivings as to his competence made certain progress in extending Britannia's rule. He first obtained signatures of all male residents at Puerto Soledad to an agreement honoring British law and regulations, and he then extended British control over the fisheries by proclaiming a three-mile inshore waters jurisdiction. Though Lowcay lacked Smith's zeal for farming and grazing he, too, left the islands in a better, more productive state than he had found them. Imperial progress in these latitudes was that of the inch-worm.

The Lords of the Admiralty also determined to support British interests in the Falklands by extending the surveys of Captain FitzRoy and of completing them as soon as possible. In 1838 H.M.'s cutter *Arrow*, Commander B. J. Sulivan, was sent to the Falklands to continue FitzRoy's admirable and pioneering work. The first mate's account of this survey, Lauchlan Bellingham Mackinnon's volume, published in London in 1840 as *Some Account of the Falkland Islands from Six Months' Residence* in 1838 and 1839, provided a glowing advertisement of the value of the Islands as a naval base. The Falklands were portrayed as the 'pivot of trade' between Australia and the Pacific littoral. They were described as the key to the commerce of those distant shores, and even the Gibraltar of the Pacific, and of the Australian seas.[38] Sulivan did his best to promote the Falklands, too, and as with others facing half-pay idleness, Sulivan had decided to make a go of it in the Falklands. He thought it the healthiest place in the world, and so keen was he to get there that he asked his wife 'Can you be ready to start for the Falklands on Thursday?' 'No', she replied, 'but I will by Monday next.' They were there until 1851, and their son, christened Falkland, is believed to be the first British subject born there. But as to the political value of the Falklands, this distinguished surveyor and naval officer compiled reports that formed some of the earliest published comment on the Falklands.[39]

By this time the government had come, if belatedly and reluctantly, to the conclusion that keeping a resident and guard on the Falkland Islands was insufficient to protect British interests. Moreover this was a time of experimentation in the modes of British colonization overseas. Assisted schemes of emigration were being developed, and the scheme for the transportation of convicts was under review. Colonial self-government was being pressed for in the colonies of settlement. And the Treasurery was noted for its penny-pinching parsimony.

As regards to the Falkland Islands the government no longer feared any Argentine military intervention. They did worry about irregular 'squatter' settlement and American depredations. A regular mode of government was merited 'on the spot', and the ministry wished to proceed with some scheme which would develop the islands and secure and enlarge British supremacy in those seas.

The scheme for the permanent settlement and advancement of national interests on the Falklands came forward in 1840, under recommendations of the Colonial Office and the Admiralty. In particular, the plan had its foundation in the advice of the Commissioners of the Colonial Land and Emigration Office given to Lord John Russell, the Secretary of State for War and the Colonies. Russell, perplexed by the status of the islands, had directed the Commissioners to peruse reports to the Admiralty from the islands describing prospects of the small settlement. With great thoroughness the Commisioners enumerated four grounds upon which the establishment of a regular colony at these islands had been urged upon government. These were, firstly, the usefulness to merchant vessels sailing round Cape Horn as a port for refit and refreshment; secondly, the expediency of having a British port placed roughly, as it were, half way between the Atlantic and Pacific oceans to which the naval forces on the South American station could resort; thirdly, the peculiar advantages which the islands afforded for the establishment of a penal colony; and, fourthly, the fitness of the islands as a settlement for agricultural and commercial purposes.[40]

With respect to the first, that of the advantage of having a British port and settlement near Cape Horn on the direct homeward passage from the western coast of South America and from the Australasian colonies, the Commissioners noted that the idea had been from time to time strongly urged. One hundred British merchants, shipowners, and traders had recently signed a request for a public meeting 'to enforce the expediency of colonizing the Falkland Islands.' The grounds of their determined position was the increase of British trade: growing numbers of ships on homeward passages were coming by way of Cape Horn instead of the Cape of Good Hope, and settlement at the islands would give facilities to whalers to refit. In addition, reports from Royal Navy officers indicated that Berkeley Sound was a desirable place to touch at for vessels from any part of the South Seas bound to Europe or North America in want of water, salt or fresh provisions or repairs. The Commissioners were heavily reliant on FitzRoy, who had considered that vessels could approach the home main island at all times with safety. All vessels coming from ports in Peru and Chile, averaging between sixty and seventy annually, all vessels coming from New Zealand, and a considerable and increasing number of vessels coming from the Australian colonies might take this way home. From New South Wales alone the number of ships clearing outwards for ports of Great Britain in the past year was 236. Whalers from London numbered up to twenty in any one year. FitzRoy had argued that homeward-bound ships from the rapidly-growing British colonies in Australia, as well as from Mexico, Peru and Chile, were in want of a port at about the middle of their voyage. Almost all ships had to 'sight' the eastern tip of the Falklands as they passed by in order to correct, or verify, their longtiude. Again, FitzRoy reasoned, if an accident occurred in doubling Cape Horn, where could a vessel go for repairs? The Rio de la Plata and Chiloé on the other side were each 1200 miles from Cape Horn. The Falklands were the only logical choice. On the basis of these purely maritime considerations, the Commissioners recommended that a base be established.[41]

In reference to the second matter, and the advantage of possessing a base of operations for H.M. ships on the South American station, the Commissioners were reminded of the fact that the Falklands had been called from time to time 'the key to the Pacific.' Anson and Byron had insisted on their importance in time of war, for the protection of commerce and the command of adjacent seas. 'Even Dr. Johnson,' the Commissioners wrote with perception, 'who so laboriously derided that idea that any Nation could desire possession for its own sake of such "weather-beaten barrenness," admitted that no man who considered its situation 'could fail to see the advantage of a settlement there in time of war.' There were good harbours. The islands were barren of timber, but they could be supplied from the neighbouring continent, or by timber-carrying vessels coming from New Zealand. As to defending national interests and as a further argument in favour of more naval force in those seas, the Commissioners were impressed by the views of Rear-Admiral Hamond. In 1835, he had complained that British, French and American sealing vessels which frequented the islands had acted without regard to laws of propriety, and the extent of coast and the number of convenient harbours afforded them so many facilities for carrying on illegal and irregular conduct. In these circumstances it was impossible to preserve order amongst them.[42] But a strong British presence would be an altogether different matter.

On the third point, the Falklands offered all the advantages of an ideal convict colony. They had no woods, no means of escape, no aborigines, and no settlers to be contaminated. The expense of shipping convicts to the islands would be less than that to Australia. With a labour force the place could be made self-sufficient in food: vegetables would grow there; wild cattle could flourish. There was peat for fuel. FitzRoy also had approved of the idea of a penal colony there, adjacent to a harbour available for a naval base.

On the fourth and last consideration, the general fitness of the islands as a settlement for agricultural and commercial purposes, the Commissioners expressed grave doubts. Admittedly there were two hundred islands. Yet only two, East and West Falkland, were of any size. The eastern was the largest, at 130 miles long and 80 miles wide. And it had a small settlement at Puerto Soledad or Port Louis, East Falklands. In 1840 it consisted of twenty-five persons including children, most of the settlers being South American gauchos who hunted wild cattle. A lieutenant of the Royal Navy with a small vessel of war served as commandant; but the place was far from progressive or well developed, and the Senior Naval Officer who had visited the place in 1839 had reported finding the settlement in an altogether deplorable condition.[43] Though for nearly eighty years settlements had been formed in these islands by different nations, and the capabilities of the soil had been tried, not a single tree grew there. FitzRoy had rightly identified wind as the 'principal evil' in this region unmatched for its storms in winter or summer. Given this, agriculture was bound to suffer. Yet grazing land lay in the northern part of the island, where wild cattle, nearly 40,000 head, 4,000 wild horses, and even some wild hogs and goats roamed. A cod fishery and seal fishery existing off Patagonia. Though animal food and vegetables existed in abundance, all timber, corn and lime had to be importedd. Mindful of the inability of the Colonial Secretary, Lord John Russell, to provide for emigration to Canada or to Port Essington, Australia, the Commissioners did not find the prospects of a Falklands colony in any way inviting. Thus the Commissioners recommended penal settlement as a means of reducing expenses.[44]

Nonetheless, the grudging support of the Commissioners was sufficient for Russell to pursue the project. He laid aside the idea of introducing convicts as settlers, perhaps on the grounds of difficulties developing that would distract the colony from its real intent: encouraging maritime enterprise in southern seas and safeguarding sea routes and, besides, Bermuda and Norfolk Islands were receiving transported convicts. With this modification, he sent the Commissioners' scheme to the Lords

Commissioners of the Admiralty for their opinion. Their Lordships were told that the colonial government was to be supported by a vote of Parliament, and thus would not be a burden on any department of government. The 'stone-frigate era' was ending. However, the establishment was to be framed on the most economical scale, not to exceed £2,000 annually. Revenues from land sales should be divided as follows: fifty per cent devoted to sending out labourers, twenty-five percent to surveys, and twenty-five percent to genereal purposes. Their Lordships agreed with Russell, and made a further suggestion that it would be expedient for the government to provide for the preservation of the wild cattle.[45] At last a formal scheme for Falklands settlement had been adopted by the British government.

Under these more ambitious considerations, government put in place a new scheme for colonization. Even then it was not much more than a skeleton affair, always on the most economical scale, and representative of earlier ventures. On 15 January 1842 Lieutenant Richard Clement Moody, a subaltern in the Corps of Royal Engineers, an expert in imperial fortifications, landed at Puerto Soledad or Port Louis from the brig *Hebe*, holding a commission as Lieutenant-Governor. With him were a Mr. Robinson, clerk and storekeeper, two servants, a butcher, and a party of four non-commissioned officers and twelve privates of the Royal Engineers. Two of the Royal Engineers were accompanied by wives and children. The arrivals boosted the resident population from forty-five, composing no less than ten nationalities, to sixty-one.[46]

Lord John Russell's instructions to Lieutenant Richard Clement Moody, R.E., of 23 August 1841, the date of his appointment, make it clear that this was to be 'empire on the cheap.' As to the nature of Moody's powers, Russell admitted the difficulty that he would have to preside over a settlement in which British title rested on the ground of prior occupation and in such circumstances colonists carried with them the law of England.[47] But without a population to govern, neither a legislature nor a court of justice could be established, and the means of administering law and justice had to be entrusted solely to Moody. The colony was to be run on £2,000 for the first year, of which £600 was to be the governor's salary. In admitting that government was providing but meagre funds, Russell was keen to point out the patriotic obligations Moody was undertaking as governor. The national advantages of the islands were increasing, if not yet convincingly established. 'It is a growing opinion among naval and mercantile men,' Russell wrote,

> that a settlement on the Falkland Islands would be of essential service to our merchant vessels in the voyages from our more distant possessions. It may be that a mere guard, to occupy a post in the vicinity of the best harbour, is all that can be effected with advantage. It may be that a more extensive occupation by British settlers would lead to increased intercourse, and improved facilities for trade. These are questions which can only be decided by experience. It will be seen in a year or two whether the appointment of a person, with a title of authority, leads to a desire to colonise, and whether the attempt, if made by companies or individuals, is likely to prove successful.[48]

The object of government, Russell concluded his instructions to Moody, was 'to give increased protection and security to British commerce' but 'not to launch into a large expense for the sake of a mere territory contained in the Falkland Islands.' In other words, the government would take into consideration Moody's views in leading to what Russell called the 'ultimate decision of Her Majesty's government in regard to the future of the Falklands.'[49]

Even at this date, 23 August 1841, the British government had made no final decision to stay.

As an empire-builder Moody was superb, and here as in British Columbia at a later date, when he was also a lieutenant-governor, he was able to maximize the benefits and minimize the obstacles of a new strategic location. From Government House, in the Falklands, he sent lengthy and detailed reports to the Colonial Office on the state of affairs in the South Atlantic and the many prospects that the Falkland Islands offered to British subjects desirous of settling there. He concurred with the Commissioners for Crown Lands in their assessment of the value of the archipelago for merchant shipping. 'The geographical position of the islands is so convenient,' he wrote on 14 April 1842, 'the numerous harbours in them so excellent, especially the most leeward on Port William, that the advantages they could be made to afford to shipping in these seas has never failed to strike all persons who have given their attention to the subject.'[50] Right he was, for commencing with Lord Anson a long list of persons had waxed eloquently on a prospective seabase in the Falklands. French and American ships regularly called there, he noted. Masters trading round Cape Horn could be sure of assistance, provisions and repairs; beef and water were cheap, also fish and wildfowl; antiscorbutic plants, wild celery, sorrel, and spinach, were available. Then he warmed to the imperial theme. 'By vessels from the Australian colonies such a halfway post will be highly valued when the islands are better known.'[51] The present difficulty lay in prejudices. The islands were hard to find, mariners told him, and no accurate charts existed. But FitzRoy's, Sulivan's and Robinson's surveys all showed advantages of harbours of unsurpassed value. As for the resident cattle, Moody had a report from 'Colonel the Capitanz of the Gauchos,' so-called, that there were 40,000 cattle, most of them long-horned, which would be admired 'even in England.' There were magnificent big bulls, and with good horses the gauchos could do work among them, and he forecast an excellent trade in the export of beef. The Falklands political importance derived from their geography, concluded Moody, and their military advantage from their harbours, and he anticipated that they would become a useful force in the enhancing of British power on and over the seas.

Where was the colonial capital to be? Port Louis, otherwise known as Puerto Soledad, was hard to approach, and the navigation to its inner reaches was hazardous, and utterly impossible for large sailing vessels to enter. Fitz-Roy's opinion was again requested, and he advised the Hydrographer of the Admiralty, Captain Francis Beaufort, that Port William would be best. Three miles in length and about a mile wide, it was easy to access in any wind, provided good shelter, had good holding ground, possessed good drinking water, and could be approached with less doubt or risk than any other port in the islands. It lay closer to the track of ships bound round Cape Horn than any other. And he concluded, with this telling comment: 'Without easy and frequent intercourse with ships, the Falklands are not worth notice – with that they may become invaluable.'[52] Predisposed on the basis of Fitz-Roy's advice that Port William was perhaps the only suitable location to attract maritime traffic, Moody also made his own reconnaissance. He also solicited the opinions of various naval officers including Lieutenant Tyssen of H.M. ketch *Sparrow* and Lieutenant Robinson of H.M. ketch *Arrow*, Mr. Bodie, on the advantages of Port William as a port. When Captains Ross and Crozier destined for Antarctica called in 1842, Moody also consulted them. They too supported the idea of a move to Port William as it was more easy of access and had deeper water. But only grudgingly and never convincingly did Moody accept Port William as the best site, owing to the nature of the boggy ground round the port. Lord Stanley approved of the colonial capital being fixed on the south shore of Port William, and he sent instructions to move the headquarters to that place as soon as possible.[53] This was done, and in July 1844 the colonial capital was fixed at Stanley Harbour in Port William Inlet, the name Stanley superseding the older name.

Subsequently, provisions for a civil government and administration of justice were established on 11 April 1843 under a statute providing for crown colony legislation.[54] The objects were to establish a civil order and to promote further settlement. The garrison was manned first by Royal Engineers, then after 1849 by Chelsea Pensioners, and after 1856 by Royal Marines.[55] Settlers were sent from Ireland and then from Scotland where their 'habits and mode of life' promised to make them 'valuable acquisitions' in the Falklands, so imperial strategists reasoned. Moody's plan for developing the Falklands as a sheep station revealed an astute assessment of the economic resources of the islands, and under this scheme legislative authority was eventually established.[56] British warships bound for the Pacific or on detached service continued to call with provisions and supplies brought from England, Rio and Buenos Aires. Self-sufficiency seems never to have been an achievable object, despite the glowing reports of naval officers.

By contrast, the expectation of government in developing the Falklands as a colony to protect and foster navigation in those seas was well met. Dutiful customs and port officers at Port Stanley kept record of the growing volume of shipping. In the four-year period 10 May 1847 to 16 June 1851, no fewer than 124 merchantmen and eleven men-of-war had called at the port, and the number swelled annually. Of the merchantmen, which aggregated 39,485 tons, sixty-five were of British and fifty-one of American register. Most visited for purposes of watering or provisioning, of making repairs, or of servicing local colonial needs. In contrast to the merchantmen, the men-of-war arrived for repairs, refreshment, surveying or government duties.[57] These details indicated, as the Colonial Office noted in 1852 with cautious optimism, that there seemed a chance that the islands would become 'a very useful place of resort of shipping.'[58] On a limited scale progress was being made with the colonization of the islands, where by 1849 some 236 persons were resident.

On 23 December 1851 the Falkland Islands Company was chartered under British statute in order to promote commercial operations onshore and in adjacent seas. And by this measure the Colonial Office placed the economic progress of the islands in the hands of the willing corporation. The company offered free passage and accommodation, a reasonable wage, and a pension after twenty years' work for any young man willing to emigrate to the islands as a shepherd. By 1852 the Colonial Land and Emigration Commissioners (who heretofore had resolutely refused to show any enthusiasm) were prepared to remark, in rather glowing terms. 'We think that there can be no doubt that there will now be a fair prospect of those islands becoming a very useful place of resort for shipping; and we are glad to see. . . . that the vessels visiting the islands are already on the increase.'[59] The governor at the time, George Rennie, who had succeeded Moody on 15 December 1847, expressed great caution in reporting that the Falklands as a colony were making 'steady though not very rapid progress.'[60]

In all of this very serious colony-making there were sometimes humorous references to the Falkland Islands reaching London from the South Atlantic. One recorded episode comes from the pen of John Macgillivray, naturalist to H.M. surveying vessel *Rattlesnake*, which put into Port Stanley in 1849 homeward bound from Torres Strait. It had been a cold and bleak passage for officers and crew, and the prospect of the dreary landscape did little to raise their spirits, save for the sight of cattle herds on shore which immediately conjured up visions of hot roast beef. Port Stanley appeared as a small straggling village of wooden houses and boasted a population of 300, of whom thirty were pensioned soldiers. Of the pensioners, Macgillivray said, they were all Irish and they appeared to be in anything but comfortable circumstances though they were paid the same as labourers, three shillings a day. One of them who had served previously in Van Diemen's Land said he often envied the lot of a convict there, for, as he put it in his distinctly Irish tongue, 'sure we are fretting to death to think that we have come to this in our old age after serving our king and country so long.' All of them complained of being deluded by highly-coloured reports of the productiveness of a colony where grain would not ripen and which had not been found 'capable of producing a tolerable potato.'[61]

The Irish asides notwithstanding, the signs for colonial development appeared promising. As the nineteenth century drew on, the Company experienced moderate success, and the Falklands grew as a sheep and cattle station. Steam navigation gave the place a new imperial value as a coal depôt. On 8 December 1914 in the Battle of the Falkland Islands the trumped-up value of Britain having mastery of those seas by possession of Anson's key to the Pacific was at last realized, though it was only the superiority of British men-of-war, particularly the battle-cruisers *Invincible* and *Inflexible*, which resulted in the decisive victory over the Imperial German Navy's squadron led by Vice-Admiral Graf von Spee. And with this triumph came an end to German cruiser warfare, and, outside of the narrow seas, England held undisputed control of the ocean trade routes of the world. In a very real way the utility of the Falklands to Britannia's rule was demonstrated.

# CHAPTER 7

# South Atlantic Empire and Diplomacy

The British were led to reassert their authority in the Falkland Islands by reoccupation in 1832 and 1833 for two reasons: the pressure of rival powers, Argentina and the United States, and the threat that the control of the Falklands might have in foreign hands to British seaborne and political interests in South America and southern oceans. Successive First Lords of the Admiralty beginning with Anson had urged the islands' occupation and development in order to enhance British maritime paramountcy and to check rival threats. Successive Secretaries of State at the Foreign Office had kept a wary eye on any encroachment that might threaten the legitimacy of British claims to sovereignty no matter how fragile. They were reluctant to expand formal British occupation. Yet in the end they were forced to intervene to secure the national interests. Despite the resistance of various statesmen, including the Duke of Wellington in 1829, Admiralty and Foreign Office opinions were strong enough to direct the course of British policy towards that of maintaining sovereignty by forceful intervention and, eventually, by colonization.

In the years after Waterloo the British government exercised the preemptive impulse in many other distant spots on the globe besides the Falklands – in Western Australia, New Zealand, British Columbia, among others. Malacca, temporarily ceded to the Dutch in 1818, was regained in 1824 in return for British withdrawal from Sumatra. In 1824 Sir Stamford Raffles established himself permanently in Singapore. In 1841 Sir James Brooke was appointed Rajah of Sarawak by the Sultan of Brunei, and in 1846 Britain acquired Labuan by cession from the Sultan for a coaling station in those seas. Aden was occupied by the British in 1839 to protect the British route to India. The Kuria Murias near Muscat, Perim, and the Cocos-Keelings, on the Australian route – were added for coaling or cable stations. And even in east Asia, Britain needed an island if the Chinese would acquiesce to fair trade demands; accordingly, in 1839 Palmerston had issued orders to take possession of some island on the China coast that would serve as a place of rendezvous and as a basis of operations. Eventually, Hong Kong was declared a British free port in 1841.[1] Almost always, as these examples demonstrate, the British preferred to annex or occupy islands, especially ones lying adjacent to continents of great commercial promise. Onshore involvement would have been troublesome and expensive. In other words, in the round-the-globe supremacy of the British Empire the Falkland Islands were but one insular base in the network of administration, security and control.

All over the world, Lord Melbourne, the prime minister complained in 1841, the British were being pestered with the 'fatal necessity' of intervening to secure their own interests, principally that of maintaining their trade and strength at sea, naval and mercantile.[2] And in the case of the Falkland Islands they had done just that. In doing so they gave credence to the wry observation of the 'Little Englander', Canon Sydney Smith, that the British maintained garrisons 'on every rock in the ocean where a cormorant could perch.'[3] 'On that dreary, desolate, windy spot, where neither corn nor trees can grow, long wisely abandoned by us,' concluded Sir William Molesworth in his attack in Parliament on British military stations overseas, 25 July 1848, 'we have, since 1841, expended upwards of £35,000; we have a civil establishment there at a cost of £5,000 a year, a Governor who has erected barracks and other "necessary" buildings well loop-holed for musketry; and being hard up for cash he issued a paper currency, not, however, with the approbation of the Colonial Office. What I propose to the House is this: to acknowledge the claims of Buenos Ayres to the Falkland Islands.'[4]

The Falklands, desolate and seemingly detached from the great currency of world affairs, invited the derision of many. Such objections by the public, more particularly by the critics of the government, more especially of its rather despised agent the Colonial Office against the growing obligations of the British nation overseas, were stated in the informed periodicals of the day. They widely advertised the perceived uselessness of the Falklands and the increased liabilities and costs to the taxpayer. 'They ought to be called Isles of Relief,' one writer opined with more than a touch of truth, but 'official management makes them deserve to be called Isles of Misfortune.'[5] The colonial administration in the Falklands came in for heavy rebuke, too. These views, it need hardly be said, continued well into the twentieth century. They became manifest in the era when the process of British decolonization found its greatest obstacles in locations virtually devoid of an economically self-sufficient and militarily-secure population.

The Falkland Islands, the former resident Whitington insisted in 1840, appeared to have 'shared the fate *of an estate in chancery with a defective title.*' That is, whilst the suit proceeded the estate was allowed 'to run to waste.'[6] The islands had decayed in ruin while England, Spain, and France had contended for the right of sovereignty. Captain

Onslow of the *Clio*, who had re-established British supremacy, had precisely the same view. 'I am astonished the Government do not colonize them,' he complained to Whitington, 'and make them a great naval depot. My dispatches clearly pointed out their importance and advantage as a station and place of refuge.'[7]

Long after Britannia's rule had been exercised by H.M.S. *Clio* in the Falkland Islands the interests of the nation in those seas and the progress of the colony continued in a perilous state. Nearly 8,000 miles distant from the home islands, the Falklands hardly merited much except derision. In the era when the prophets of 'Little England' preached a reduction of colonial responsibilities, the Falklands remained a constant drain on the Treasury.

The case of the Falkland Islands demonstrates a number of characteristics of British imperialism in the early nineteenth century. First, after a long phase of apparent inaction, indifference, and neglect the British government intervened. Foreign threats necessitated intervention, and commercial primacy was inseparable from naval security. What statesmen and strategists regarded in 1815 as unnecessary spots of advantage in the South Atlantic had become by 1832 places of national necessity. Second, during the reign of William IV, British policy-makers continued to wrestle with how to maintain an advantage on and over the seas in the face of rivals for trade or dominion. This was not an age of imperial neglect, or of mere preoccupation with slavery or aborigines issues. Rather, it was an era when imperial accessions did occur but only where commercial advantage and naval benefit would accrue to the Empire. An analysis of Hawaiian or Society Islands history, or that of Fernando Po, Hong Kong, or the Northwest Coast of North America would be equally illustrative of the theme that economic security, maritime enterprise, and naval needs went hand in hand. Third and last, British strength depended on trade advantage over other rivals, and that depended in turn on possessing spots of distant oceans for economic advantage, protection of commerce, and, in consequence, naval security. Thus from among one of the most neglected periods of British imperial history we are able to learn the maxim of imperialism for much of the nineteenth century: Profit and power went hand in hand, and when necessary British governments would *annex* territories, or in the case of the Falkland Islands *reoccupy* them. This did involve expensive schemes of colonization which parsimonious policy-makers sought to keep to a minimum, or otherwise place in the hands of chartered companies and settlement associations.

England had permanent interests to defend, and from 1815 to 1914 throughout the age of *Pax Britannica* those interests required intervention to secure trade or territory whenever necessary. Such a policy would garner under the Union Jack not just a few rocky barren wind-swept islets in the South Atlantic. In due course it would add much of the continent of Africa, the Antipodes, and of northern North America besides. The high tide of late-Victorian imperialism had already begun to rise first a half century or more before. In the end it is the continuities in policy-making, not the variations or departures of the laissez-faire, free-trade era which ought to be remembered.

The Falkland Islands remained within the empire as a colony or a dependency.[8] There were fundamental, inter-locking reasons for this: they were never economically self-sufficient, they never have had a large enough popula-tion or exchequer to enjoy any prospect of a *secure* nation-hood, and they were adjacent to an aggressive nation once ousted from their territory by British force. On the British side, the empire continued for equally clear reasons: official British policy held the view, never abandoned, that British citizens merited British protection, that Britain would never sacrifice the rights of the 'kelpers' to live under the flag of their own choosing, and that if the Falkland Islanders wished independence then they should have it, as forty-nine other states had done already in letting loose Mother's apron strings.

What British ministries underestimated, however, was the danger of foreign interference. Thus in the 1820s they knew almost nothing about Argentine encroachments and American sloop diplomacy until it was too late. Even after reasserting their sovereignty in 1832-3 they were uncertain as to how they should protect their holding, and how much that protection might cost. Thus in an era of rigid economics they scaled down their establishment at their peril, but not before they were obliged by a vote of Parliament to spend much more than they had ever expected or hoped.

In Britain, empire was discounted in value, but in Argentina sovereign territory had to be redeemed. Argentina never gave up its hopes of regaining its *terra irredenta*. Their historians continued to recite the eighteenth-century history of the islands, and to stress that Argentina was the legal heir to Spanish sovereign claims. Argentine rights were and are substantial. 'The simple geographical, historical and legal truths, without any exaggerations,' wrote Rear-Admiral Laurio Destéfani, 'constitute the best defence of our rights of sovereignty over the three Southern archipelagoes (the Falklands, South Georgia and South Sandwich groups) and the Cormoran and Negra rocks (the Auroras).'[9] In his view, the three archipelagoes must be Argentine because the cause is just. The Malvinas were, according to this view, Spanish until 1811 and consequently Argentine by inheritance. Particularly galling to Argentine historians is the fact that the islands were, as Destéfani words it, 'usurped by Great Britain in a time of peace and friendship with our country.'[10]

Britain was regarded as robber, and an illegal usurper. And on the borders of Argentina there had been constant haggles too – a war with Brazil ending in the new country of Uruguay, a bounday settlement with Paraguay in 1878, and quarrels with Chile leading to frontier settlements.

Argentine protests dating from 1833[11] contain the same content. In 1841 Moreno filed an official complaint against British actions; for his part Aberdeen considered the matter closed.[12] Moreno persisted in 1849. But the Foreign Office did not waver and Palmerston, Aberdeen's successor, politely declined.[13] The impasse continued.[14] British Foreign and Commonwealth secretaries wear the mantle of Aberdeen and of Palmerston.

The United States, frequently the silent partner in the South Atlantic triangle, found themselves playing two roles: that of predominant power in the Americas and that of a defender of the legal position of the British. Secretary of State Daniel Webster's view, 1841, was that until Britain and Argentina patched up their differences, the United States could not consider Argentina's demands for an indemnification for the *Lexington* raid.[15] This was enshrined as State Department policy. Nevertheless, as Secretary of State Thomas Bayard advised Argentine Minister Vincente Quesada in 1886, even if Argentina could demonstrate it possessed the rightful title to sovereignty 'there would not be wanting ample ground upon which the conduct of Captain Duncan in 1831 could be defended.'[16] Sympathetically, the American public might be seen in more recent times to defend seemingly oppressed Latin Americans against imperial England; yet little known or appreciated, was the fact that the State Department had first backed the British position in 1832, had defended that view in several sequels during the nineteenth and twentieth centuries, and was not likely to make any major departures from the official line if Argentina should invade the British–held Falkland Islands.

Britain would have preferred to let the issue die. The matter would not go away. The Argentine claim may have been flimsy but the British claim was not legally flawless.[17] Palmerston's view was that it was 'very unadvisable' to revive 'a correspondence which had ceased by the acquiescence of one of the parties and the maintenance of the other.'[18] He underestimated the Argentine official memory, its reliance on history, the chains of the past.

The Argentine government took up the issue once again in 1884 and for the next fifteen years persisted in dogging British foreign secretaries in London and ambassadors in Buenos Aires on the matter. In 1884 Dr. Ortiz, the Argentine minister for foreign affairs, in a conversation informed Edmund Monson, H.M.'s minister at Buenos Aires, that Argentina was 'rounding off' its territories and intended to revive its claim to the Malvinas. Dr. Ortiz thought the matter might be resolved by arbitration.[19] Monson warned the Governor of the Falkland Islands, and the official line as returned to the Argentine minister was that H.M.'s government would not permit any infringement on their sovereignty; to this was added bluntly that, in their view, nothing good could arise from any attempt at reopening the question.[20]

Dr. Ortiz responded violently to the British position. The republic could not but regard the islands as both naturally and legally part of the republic: 'naturally by reason of their geographical position, and legally as part of her inheritance from the mother country.'[21] The Argentine government intended to show the Falklands as Argentine territory on a forthcoming official map. The same government also held the view that the Secret Understanding between Great Britain and Spain was the means of acknowledging Spanish title, Monson replied that unless documents could be produced there was no pretext for such an argument and he even went so far as to suggest that no such Secret Understanding had ever been entered into.[22] 'What really appeared to Mr Monson to be the strong point in the Argentine case,' wrote the Foreign

Office analyst, 'was the history of the period between 1774 and 1810, from which it clearly seemed that during that time Spain exercised rights of sovereignty over the islands without any protest being made by Great Britain.'[23] Ortiz had been careful to include this emphasis in his own memorandum.[24]

The Secretary of State for Foreign Affairs, Lord Granville, was placed in a bit of a quandry. He did not want to open what might be a pandora's box. Granville's view was that Britain had been in undisputed possession for fifty years or so, and it was his position that no answer would be given and no further discussion on the subject, verbally or in writing, be carried on.[25] In turn Lord Rosebery and Lord Salisbury were pestered on the same issue. Britain's man in Buenos Aires, now Francis Pakenham, was under severe pressure, especially when he conveyed the Salisbury ruling: the discussion was closed.[26] The Argentine government protested, giving the usual reasons; Pakenham merely acknowledged receipt of the communication.[27] Again the Argentine government responded by saying that Britain's refusal did not impair Argentina's rights of sovereignty.[28] Yet again this issue had gone back and forth without satisfaction to Argentina.

For a time the matter lay dormant but in 1906 the Argentine Government took charge of the meteorological station on South Orkneys with the express sanction of the British Government.[29] The Argentine government then argued this as a claim to sovereignty, and the British ambassador was instructed to inform them categorically that the group in question was British territory.[30]

The British minister in Buenos Aires, Walter Townley, disliked the fact that Argentina had been permitted rights of running the South Orkneys weather post. 'I would respectfully venture to submit,' he wrote Sir Edward Grey at the Foreign Office on 5 October 1910, 'that the disputed ownership of the barren rocks may possibly some day lead to an unpleasant incident.'[31] The longer the Argentine flag waved over the islands the more plausible and more popular would the Argentine claim to possession become. Added anxieties would ensue, and a possible dispute. He concluded with clear understanding of the issues: 'The possession of the Falklands Islands is always dragged in at the tail of the South Orkeys, and some bombastic language is indulged in as to what Argentina will do when she has a large fleet and one hundred and fifty million inhabitants, but reasonable people have given up hope that Great Britain will ever consent to a discussion of this question.'[32]

The official British view was one of stern opposition to either admitting any difficulties with the legality of the claim or of entering into any further discussion. The Foreign Office knew, however, that the vessel was not water-tight. In 1910, Gerald Spicer, a clerk at the Foreign Office minuted that the question of the ownership of the Falklands was still not resolved. He had before him on his desk Gaston de Bernhardt's exhaustive, 49-page Confidential Print entitled *Memorandum Respecting the Falkland Islands*.[33] 'For more than 60 years we have refused to discuss the question with the Argentine Gov[ernment],' Spicer wrote, 'but from a perusal of this memo, it is difficult to avoid the conclusion that the Argentine Govt's attitude is not altogether unjustified, and that our action has been somewhat high-handed. If the alleged secret understanding between the Spaniards and ourselves could be traced our claims would probably be found to be weaker than they are.'[34] To his way of thinking, the Foreign Office position ought to be that caution should be exercised in raising with the Argentine government any questions regarding the South Orkneys or South Georgia. He added with a glance at the future: 'whatever we may have said at different times, the Argentine Govt do not regard this question as closed.'[35]

# CHAPTER 8

# Unfinished Business

At the outset of the twentieth century the Falklands had come to enjoy a favourable economic circumstance. No longer could the islands be classified as objects of relief dependent on London. For they had become an outpost of the British Empire whose values of export were far in excess of the values of import. In fact, as the nineteenth century had proceeded the archipelago had witnessed growing profitability. Under the auspices of the Falkland Islands Company lucrative trades in wool and canned meat, fish, seal and whale oils, and associated products, had turned what many well informed individuals thought an economic liability into a remarkable profit-making concern.

On the eve of the First World War this cluster of islands supported nearly three-quarters of a million sheep. Truly this land, which was 'in the main a wild stretch of moorland,' had become 'practically one large sheep run.'[1] The climate suited sheep, and the turf had productive results. Wool accounted for seven-eighths of the colony's exports; sheep-skins and tallow constituted the remaining items. The domestic economy was almost entirely devoted to sheep raising and dependent trades. Sheep were primarily bred for wool but there was an ancillary trade in meat canning. These trades were to flourish and to grow.

The second-ranking industry of the Falklands in the early twentieth century was whaling. The enterprises of the Enderbys and of Fanning formed but a curtain-up to the main act: as the nineteenth century progressed whalers had reached farther north into the Pacific. In the Southern Ocean they had similarly expanded their activities. By the early twentieth century various scientific expeditions to the South Orkneys, to the east coast of Antarctica, and to the west coast, at Graham Land, new grounds for hunting the cachelot had been disclosed, and new harbours to secure marine products too. Oil production therefore developed at bases in the Falklands and South Georgia. The South Sandwich Islands were visited by the whalers, too. As it turned out the Dependencies of the Falklands, a new oceanic empire based on the governor's house and harbour at Port Stanley, was to possess a whaling industry greater than that of the rest of the world put together. In the 1920-21 season, for instance, 5247 whales were caught, the landed value of which, in oil, was £1,250,000. So valuable was this branch of commerce that the Falkland Islands Government acquired Robert Falcon Scott's old command, the Antarctic vessel *Discovery*, with a view to learning more of the numbers and habits of the whale. Conservation of a declining stock was the object, for the sad lesson of whaling had been the practical extermination of whales where they had been heavily hunted.[2]

The whaling industry, of which Port Stanley became the nexus, had the valuable by product of boosting the marine industries of the Falklands. Ship repair and refit, fueling, provisioning and watering grew into sizeable industries engaging most of the workers. In 1912 eighty-eight steamers and twelve sailing vessels called at Port Stanley. Ship condemning was a popular industry too. Still, sheepraising held a major place on the colonial accounts where exports and imports were tallied and policy-makers were always mindful of the sheep-raising character of the colonists, who were mainly of Scottish descent. In 1914, the Falklands' population stood at 2,772. Another thousand were in the Dependencies. Of the total, half had been born locally and were known as 'kelpers'. Less than forty percent of the population was female. The number of foreigners had risen dramatically in the previous decade. Norwegians and Swedes active in whaling found Port Stanley a useful base of operations. But sheep remained king, and the population reflected that. In the words of a scientific observer, commenting on the sociological change of the Falklands since the mid-nineteenth century: 'These thrifty people have entirely replaced the early South American settlers and gauchos, and with them have vanished the wild cattle and horses, which were less profitable than sheep.'[3]

While the progress of this island empire advanced incrementally and without interruption a new change was coming over the waters and over the affairs of the British islands in the Southern Hemisphere. The British government, and the colonial governor at Port Stanley, W.L. Allardyce, had long worried about the depleting stock of whales. Accordingly, in 1908, colonial waters were to be closely policed against whalers not possessing licences, and the local Colonial Secretary was empowered to grant such licences for whatever terms and conditions in respect of the number and tonnage of vessels to be employed in the taking of whales.[4] That meant that the Governor was the master of all that he surveyed or chose to survey.

In that same year the United Kingdom, under letters patent, appointed the Governor of the Colony of the Falkland Islands to be Governor of South Georgia, the South Orkneys, the South Shetlands, the Sandwich Islands and Graham Land, Antarctica.[5] The sector of Falkland Islands Dependencies now boasted an aggregate land mass of one million square miles. Between longitude $20^\circ$ west and $80^\circ$ west south of $50^\circ$ south, this sector, with the South Pole as its apex, constituted a very big pie, an imperial slice as it were. The Governor's original fiat to police the whaling in Falklands' waters now ran throughout the Dependencies.[6] The Whale Fishery Ordinance, as the document is known, now enabled London and Port Stanley to rule the waves – constitutionally at least. The British claims were recognized by Norway, the main whaling rival, by Argentina, by Chile, and by other powers.[7]

Such developments in imperial water and resource management also had their origins in a threat to British dominion, and they came from a surprising, unexpected source. In 1904, a Norwegian, Captain L.E. Larsen, decided to fish the South Atlantic for whales and to establish a shore whaling station at South Georgia. His company was formed in Buenos Airies and carried the name Compañia Argentina de Pesca. But this problem was to be compounded, for in the following year a Chilean company under the grand title of the South Georgia Exploration Company, financed by Chilean-based British capital, attended on the Government at Port Stanley and were granted a mining and grazing lease of South Georgia. Empires were about to collide. The Chileans sailed to South Georgia only to find Larsen's Compañia Argentina de Pesca in possession of the very best site. As it turned out the Captain had applied through the English legation in Buenos Aires for a whaling license for South Georgia. Faced with such a conundrum, the British government had only one resource: 'send a gun-boat!' The protected cruiser H.M.S. *Sappho*, Commander Michael Hodges, was sent to investigate matters. The officer commanding interrogated the Norwegians. He told them, according to one source, that they had no business to be there.[8] The Norwegians hotly disputed this. Captain Hodges insisted that the Norwegian flag be lowered but the manager vehemently protested. Under threat that the Norwegian flag would be shot down within fifty minutes if not taken down, the

Norwegian whalers thought the better of their position and pulled down their colours.[9] A more recent history, disputes the threatening nature of the encounter. 'Some conflicting accounts,' writes Robert Headland, '. . . suggest that there was either a Norwegian or Argentine flag flying over Grytviken (in South Georgia) to which Hodges objected, that Hodges gave Larsen a time (said to be either 15 or 30 minutes) to remove the flat before *Sappho's* guns, trained on the flag pole, would open fire to the same effect, and that Larsen lowered the offending flag. Neither the official account prepared by Captain Hodges nor the Norwegian histories refer to this and no supporting contemporary reports include it.'[10] The action, real or imagined, is embedded in the mythology of South Georgia's history. 'All other accounts,' concludes the authority on these things, 'indicate that relations between Captain Hodges and Larsen were amicable and cooperative.'[11]

This event was doubtless what historians would like to call the immediate cause of the constitutional provisions that enlarged British sovereignty and obligation in the Southern Ocean. But there were larger issues afoot. For one, this was an era of intense imperial rivalry, when all the sundry spots of earch and water were being grabbed to prevent them falling within the group of rival powers. The imperial scramble, so vital in African affairs, had now reached the islands of South Atlantic and the Antarctic continent. Imperial impulses were quickening here as elsewhere. No vacant lands or islets, shores or continents remained free from the entanglements of the European quests for power, gain and security. A second, more long-range factor was the desire to control the economic affairs of the Falklands and its dependencies. Conservation measures, founded in justifiable fears had led government to mount major scientific expeditions. Such expeditions, as noted, enlarged the world's knowledge about where whales might be found and where shore bases for extracting oil might be established. Commerce followed science in this case, and the flag followed trade. For a third, south polar exploration was advancing as quickly as geographical societies, benefactors, sponsors, subscribers, and boards of admiralty could make up their minds as to requirements and resources, 'cost-sharing' and 'spheres of influence.[12] And expedition instructions had to be readied. 'The Antarctic region may be another Klondyke,' the Norwegian Carsten Borchgrevik, the first man to winter in Antarctica, advised the *Westminster Gazette*.[13] He added that fisheries might be established, a complement to the other maritime activities of European nations interested in these seas.[14] Such statements made good copy in the nationally-spirited press, and they speeded the process of exploration and, in turn, of Port Stanley's prominence in world affairs.

The great war brought a change to the permissive policy of allowing foreigners to whale in these waters. Whale oil was a strategic commodity, and the British government adopted measures to prevent neutral nations exporting such oils from whence they could be sold to Germany. A 1915 ordinance prohibited the export of whale oil except to the United Kingdom.[15]

The Norwegians, it may be noted, had a special interest in these affairs. Numerous Norwegian whaling companies took out British licenses, and they almost always complied with the laws of the Falkland Islands Government. Many years later, at the International Court of Justice in 1956, the British argued that these facts established by implication Norway's recognition of British sovereignty over the Dependencies in and about 1908. In 1938, by a Norwegian proclamation, the western frontier of Norway's own Antarctic claim coincided happily with the eastern boundary of the Falkland Islands Dependencies.[16]

Argentina did not have the same view of what they regarded as British encroachments in their rightful domain of land and water. They had never accepted the British reconquest of the Falklands. They took umbridge at the fact that the British Empire had now extended its tentacles to grasp South Georgia. In 1917 the British government, having thrown away all back-tracking arguments on the subject, issued supplemental Letters Patent on 28 March 1917 to reconfirm the boundaries of the Dependencies as 'all islands and territories whatsoever between the 20th degree of West longitude and the 50th degree of West longitude which are situated south of the 50th parallel of South latitude; and all islands and territories whatsoever between the 50th degree West longitude and the 80th degree of West longitude which are south of the 58th parallel of South latitude.'[17]

This geographical jumble of words meant that Britain had reaffirmed claims to existing islands and lands of the Dependency, and they sought to make clear to other nations these claims: moreover, they intended to make provision for the exercising of authority on and over this watery world. The Falklands, too, was becoming an outpost of Britain's Antarctic empire.

In spite of Britain's open assumption of sovereignty, the clear definition of boundaries, and the exercise of authority throughout the Falklands Islands Dependencies, Argentina 'formulated pretensions', to use a Foreign Office term.[18] They did so in 1925 to the South Orkneys, in 1927 to South Georgia as well as to the South Orkneys, and in 1937 to *all* the territories of the Falkland Islands Dependency.[19] A legal war had been declared. But it was always the Foreign Office's view that not only did British authority exist throughout the Dependencies but that scientific expeditions had anchored British claims to sovereignty. Always to be remembered, as the Foreign Office argument ran, was the fact that, in that office's irreplaceable words, 'during the years at the beginning of the present century, when Great Britain was confirming and consolidating her ancient titles to the Dependencies, Norway, the state principally interested in Antarctic whaling, and Argentina and Chile, made no reservations in regard to Great Britain's display and exercise of state activity in those territories.'[20] The Foreign Office also pointed out at the International Court of Justice in 1915 that these facts also showed that Norway, Argentina and Chile recognized British sovereignty over the Dependencies.[21] Besides which, no other nation during this period uttered a whimper of protest against the British claims.[22]

The Foreign Office, as the 1930s advanced, had the very decided view that the Argentine government was manufacturing a claim to the Dependencies. In 1934 the Argentine government authorized funding to translate Paul Groussac's sympathetic *Les Iles Malouines* into Spanish. The next year two persons born in the Malvinas were ordered to be given Argentine birth certificates. In 1936 Argentina issued a postage stamp showing the islands coloured as Agentine territory. Sir Anthony Eden, Foreign Secretary, remarked that such a postage stamp could only be detrimental to good relations between the two governments and reiterated that H.M.'s government could not admit any such claims to the Falklands. Carlos Saavedra Lamas, Argentina's foreign minister, made clear that 'the monetary solution' of the problem might remain but that Argentina would look for a final solution. 'In other words,' wrote the legal historian Gordon Ireland in 1936 'Argentina would wait and watch and do nothing rash at present but seize the first favourable opportunity for putting on the pressure for recognition of her claims when next she would have Great Britain in a tight spot for bargaining, over some diplomatic slip or desired trade concession.'[23]

The diplomatic question now became enlarged. In 1937 the Argentine ambassador in London advised the Foreign Office that Argentina reserved the rights claimed to sovereignty over the Dependencies. 'The Ambassador's *démarche*,' argued London, 'was the first intimation of an Argentine claim not merely to South Georgia and the South Orkneys *but to all the territories of the Falkland Islands Dependencies*.'[24] This 'progressive and deliberate' character of the Argentine invasion of British rights was clearly evident to the Foreign Office, and the Foreign Secretary expressly declared that the Argentine reservation could in no way affect British rights to the Falklands Islands Dependencies,[25] precisely Palmerston's reply to Ambassador Moreno's similar claim nearly a century before. The Foreign Office with the narrow and clear-sighted position that some have dismissed as arrogant and others would understand as well-reasoned put it this way to the International Court of Justice in 1956:

> The methods (of which some account has just been given) by which Argentina sought between 1925 and 1938 to advance pretensions to the sovereignty of the Falkland Islands Dependencies were not those to be expected of a State already having sovereignty, and relying upon prior and well-established legal titles. They were rather those of a State seeking gradually to manoeuvre another State out of its possession and rights. Instead of actively displaying and exercising its authority in and in regard to the territories of the Dependencies in accordance with their circumstances, the Argentine Government merely attempted by diplomatic moves to throw doubt upon the existing British titles. [26]

For some years the international struggle for the Falklands remained dormant, for neither Argentina nor Chile sought to enter a counter-claim against Britain at the International Court of Justice. There the matter stood; meanwhile, the battle was commenced in the General

Assembly of the United Nations. In 1965 the General Assembly approved a resolution inviting Britain and Argentina to hold discussions on the vexatious matter. The intent was to find a peaceful solution to the problem. The two governments engaged in diplomatic dialogue, and in 1970 delegations of the two powers met in London. The interests of the Islanders had always been of concern, one hates to say paramount concern, to Whitehall, but participants from the Falklands attended the summit meeting. Argentina had for some years placed a nasty ban on direct communications between the South American mainland and the Falklands. The 1970 talks, and those of the next year in Buenos Aires, led to the happy agreement whereby air and sea communications, postal services, custom measures, and educational and medical facilities for Islanders in Buenos Aires were effected.[27] A new state of cooperation had come into being. The Foreign Office historian of these developments, in a slight of hand completely denying any thoughts of decolonization, that is to say liquidation of an imperial asset or liability, remarks that 'the British Government were keen that such practical links between Argentina and the islands should grow as their future welfare and development would clearly be best assured with Argentine cooperation.'[28] The two states did not stop there, and in 1974 went on to sign agreements on facilitating trade and conveyance of goods between the islands and the mainland and enabling the Argentine state petroleum company to sell their wares in the Falklands.[29] Indeed, gigantic strides had been made in South Atlantic affairs and this bode well for the future, or so the participants thought.

The British government were quite agreeable to all of this and happily kept up the communication. The South Atlantic gales had quite swept away with the passage of time, and a long contented summer seemed the quite normal state of affairs. The government looked for closer links with Argentina, ties that were good for business. Leaving the Islanders to their own devices never became the official line. But in 1976 Lord Shackleton's economic survey of the archipelago suggested by its findings, if not the predisposition of the government, that closer cooperation with Argentina was called for.[30] On this basis the British governmnent took the issue one step further and invited Argentina to consider, or to explore, an arrangement for closer economic and political cooperation. Economic cooperation had always been the aim; political cooperation was something entirely new. Working groups busied themselves studying the issue of sovereignty and political accord, at the same time commercial relations were under discussion. Talks took place in 1980 and then again in February 1981, this time in New York.[31]

By this time Argentina had made it clear that the British view that there should be a 'freeze' on the disputed question of sovereignty for an agreed period of time (while, meanwhile, closer economic ties were nurtured) was totally unacceptable.[32] The Argentine position seems to have been that the British were stalling. Buenos Aires demanded action. In February 1982 formal talks took place in New York, again with Islanders represented. The parties agreed to find a solution to the dispute and the British agreed to study an Argentine proposal for new procedures, procedures designed to facilitate progress.[33]

These diplomatic niceties reflect the bankruptcy of the two parties at this stage. It is true that negotiations were in progress when Argentina invaded South Georgia in March and the islands on 2 April, and this gives a lie to the argument that war is diplomacy by other means. But British policy had not budged on the question of sovereignty, though thoughts of a co-dominion might be pondered. Whitehall had good signs of a change in the wind. '. . . in recent months,' wrote the Foreign Office historian just after the invasion, 'the Government had been aware of a number of indications that the Argentine Government was adopting a more threatening attitude towards the Falkland Islands.'[34] Such a position was not unprecedented, the same authority continued, for the dispute had been smouldering for years 'and by no means all the indicators, diplomatic and military, suggested that the dispute was about to enter an entirely new phase.'[35] The government did not enter *surprise* into its diplomatic equation, and it trusted to equitable arrangements for the future.

'We have absolutely no doubt about our sovereignty,' said Mrs Margaret Thatcher, the Prime Minister, in the House of Commons the day after the Argentine flag was run up at Port Stanley. She stated that British sovereignty had been continuous since 1833. 'Equally,' she continued, 'we have no doubt about the unequivocal wishes of the Falkland Islanders, who are British in stock and tradition, and wish to remain British in allegiance. We cannot allow the democratic rights of the Islanders to be denied by the territorial ambitions of Argentina.'[36]

On that very same day, the United Nations Security Council passed a resolution demanding an immediate withdrawal of Argentine forces, and the very same resolution called for the two governments to seek a diplomatic solution to the crisis.[37]

In the affairs of nations the search for security and individual advantage has always been matched by the necessities, or the intentions, of making an enduring international peace. At all times British policy aimed at security for the home islands and distant dependencies, economic prosperity for the nation, and regulated order in those parts of the world where the Union Jack flew or where British interests were paramount. Such intentions for the benefits of peace, prosperity and order always rested on the state of international affairs, and on the equilibrium of states and the quiescence of rivals. Every British attempt towards these ends was advanced against a backdrop of international rivalry and of uncertainty over which the British could have no expectation of controlling.

The history of the Falklands or Malvinas over three centuries shows a changing set of circumstances over time. During the eighteenth century Britain's rival claimants were France and Spain. In the nineteenth century, Argentina came forward, upon recognition of its emergence from the moribund Spanish empire there, to challenge British ascendance in the Falklands. In the twentieth century Argentina's policy was continued and intensified. As British imperial claims enlarged themselves to include South Georgia, South Sandwich, South Orkneys and Antarctica, so too did competing nations including Norway and Chile come to join Argentina in questioning British hegemony in far southern latitudes.

Even so, no power challenged Britain in these seas as did feisty Argentina. Its mainly European society had inherited a strength of purpose upon independence in 1816 that was a credit to the resolve of old Imperial Spain. Argentina's ambitions for commercial advantage and territorial integrity naturally collided with British historic interests in the old 'key to the Pacific.' Strange to say Argentina took a substantial interest in the commercial prosperity and future of the archipelago at a time when the British empire in these seas was quite asleep. The Argentine claim to the Malvinas before 1833 is irrefutable in terms of actual occupation. History, however, shows no charity. For conquest in 1833 by Britain has been called a reassertion of British power. Since that year, until the violence of 1982, the local colonial population continued in peaceful possession of the islands and dependencies. Argentine ambition and nationalism was undoubtedly boundless, and for well known reasons. The economy was always dependent on European capital and markets, mainly British, and the national governments had always been beset by inflationary tendencies, debt crises, and foreign creditors. Dictatorial regimes were a common occurence, and so were democratically inspired governments who in between times, like the dictators, sought to give Argentina dignity in the community of nations. But being an ex-Spanish colony carried with it an awful price. For Argentina had to adhere to Spanish history, which it had rejected by revolution, and, at the same time, contend with a British imperial authority which was second to none in the nineteenth century and not without substantial power in the twentieth. It is not surprising then that the two powers collided; it is surprising that they did not do so more often.

Yet this problem in the history of nations was never just confined to two states. Numerous nations parade across the face of Falklands history, including, at one time or another, Dutch explorers, French colonists and mariners, and Norwegian whalers. None, however, are to be exceeded in importance as 'third party' than the Americans. Not only as sealers and whalers did they play their part. Their desires for hemispheric dominance or leadership naturally brought them into conflict with Britain or into rivalry with other powers. They had no intention of hoisting the Stars and Stripes on the Falklands; what they wanted was free, unrestricted access to its harbours and seas. In effect British imperialism gave them that. They cleared away Argentine obstructions to such measures in 1831, and they thereby facilitated a British resurgence in those seas. Thus the nation that had shaken off the British imperial yoke found itself a nominal, undeclared ally of British aspirations and imperial activities in the early nineteenth century. The Monroe Doctrine was a license of convenience for British interests when it suited Whitehall. In 1982, after indecision and attempts at peace-keeping the United States again backed the United Kingdom in regards to its territorial rights of sovereignty in those islands.

But a new change had come over these waters, one not only affecting the regional affairs of the Falklands/

Malvinas but south polar matters as widely different as Antarctic ownership and nuclear-free zones. A twelve-nation treaty, effective 1959, froze all territorial claims to Antarctica, including the overlapping claims of Argentina, Chile and the United Kingdom. This treaty stabilized claims to the continent, but it did not bring an end to turbulence over the continent's islands or to the Falklands dispute. As Lord Shackleton pointed out, Britain made several attempts to take the issue of ownership of the Antarctic territories to the International Court but Argentina and Chile refused to submit their claims. Meantime, the Argentines have flown pregnant women to its Antarctic bases to have babies born there, and Argentine cabinet meetings have been held at base Marambio. Thus from a purely geopolitical posture the Falklands is a counterweight to any threat to Antarctica's position. Thus, runs the argument, if Britain were to give up the Falklands the influence of Britain in Antarctica and in the British Antarctic Survey would be weakened. Lord Shackleton's 1982 inquiry on long-term implications worded the issue this way: 'While naturally our major concern has been the Falkland Islands and their inhabitants, we have sought to draw attention to wider and long-term issues in the South Atlantic and Antarctic. Although the Falklands are now the focus of political attention, South Georgia may in the long run be of great importance to the future developments of the potential wealth of the South-West Atlantic and the Antarctic. We also emphasize the importance of the right conservation policies, and of the need for awareness of possible threats to the Antarctic Treaty.'[38]

In short, the quarrel over the Falklands/Malvinas had become one of very much wider implications, and in an era in which the new dominion of science exercises a profound impact on world opinion and geopolitics the British Empire in Antarctica has taken on a new role, one never possibly conceived of by Lords Palmerston and Aberdeen,

Granville and Salisbury. During the 1920s the Colonial Secretary, Leo Amery, thought Britain should own all of Antarctica. Those years have passed, and formal empire is out of fashion, and now international law is the new mode of settling disputes, except when force is resorted to.

Ten years after the Argentine strike at Port Stanley, the Argentine President, Carlos Menem, and the Foreign Secretary, Guido di Tella, in what they describe as a new climate of co-operation and confidence, have suggested that the dispute might be referred to international arbitration, a rejection of Argentina's age-old policy of avoiding arbitration.[39] The Falkland Islands, meanwhile, has designated 10 January as 'Margaret Thatcher Day', a clear warning that Kelpers will not in any way accept an abandoning of their rights under the Union Jack. The fundamental questions remain, but the issues have multiplied. A new British Empire, one perhaps unwanted by some, one perhaps added, as last century's historian of imperial accessions, Sir John Seeley, would have his readers believe, in the fit of absentmindedness, has risen in the South Atlantic and in Antarctica. Meanwhile, persistent rumours of great fish stocks, mineral finds, and oil discoveries provide economic incentives, and further calls for policing and conservation measures.

Meanwhile the Falklands had gone through three phases of British imperial rule – the First Empire of rivalry with France and Spain, during which claims had been staked out against the continental rivals, the Second Empire, during which the British ran a skeletal empire in the Falklands until such time as the Falkland Islands Company advanced the true sheep and whaling interests of the archipelago, and the third or last British Empire, during which the British endeavoured to run down their estate and reach an accord with Argentina concerning the future of the island.

British Empire in the Falklands spans three centuries and may well enter a fourth. While British interests in Canada,

Australia, South Africa and elsewhere have moved through what has been assumed to be the logical rise and fall of empires, in the Falklands the interest has been, out of necessity, constant. The Falklands thus defies the usual rules of the British imperial ethos. Easily acquired, it may yet be the most difficult to dispose of. '. . . the basic question,' writes Peter Beck, the contemporary authority, on the matter with true understanding, 'is whether the area of dispute can be transformed into a factor making for cooperation between the two governments, and in a manner accepted to the islanders, rather than remain a cause for a second Malvinas War.'[40]

History knows no laws. But it does teach lessons, at least those of warning. Even the most jaded historian comes sooner or later to the understanding that 'the more things change the more they seem the same.' The Falkland Islands/Malvinas conflict demonstrates one of the continuities of history – the on-going struggle for the islands in times past. This is true whether Spain was quarreling with France or with England for the islands. This was also true whether Britain was exercising its weight in the South Atlantic when, as the opportunity afforded itself, the Argentines and Americans were disputing the rights to the fisheries of those seas. To this date, the Falklands remain one of the unravelled puzzles of human history. Equally it remains one of the unresolved problems of international affairs which merits every attention by politicians and statesmen intent on the peaceful resolution of conflict and the avoidance of war.

# Abbreviations

*(full particulars in Note on Sources and Bibliography)*

| | |
|---|---|
| Adm. | Admiralty Papers in the P.R.O. |
| *A.R.* | *Annual Register* |
| *B.F.S.P.* | *British and Foreign State Papers* |
| B.L. | British Library |
| Boyson | V.F. Boyson, *The Falkland Islands* . . . (1924) |
| Broadlands MSS | Palmerston Papers, Historical Manuscripts Commission, London |
| C.O. | Colonial Office Papers in the P.R.O. |
| *D.N.B.* | *Dictionary of National Biography* |
| Down | W.C. Down, 'The Occupation of the Falkland Islands' (1926/27) |
| *F.I.J.* | Falkland Islands Journal |
| F.O. | Foreign Office Papers in the P.R.O. |
| *H.A.H.R.* | *Hispanic American Historical Review* |
| H.D. | Hydrographic Department, Ministery of Defence (Navy), Taunton, Somerset |
| *H.J.* | *Historical Journal* |
| H.M.C. | Historical Manuscripts Commission, London |
| Goebel | Julius Goebel, Jr., *Struggle for the Falkland Islands* (1927, rep. 1982) |
| Manning | W.R. Manning, ed., *Diplomatic Correspondence. . . . Vol 1 Argentina* (1932) |
| Moore | J.B. Moore, ed., *A Digest of International Law, Vol. 1* (1906) |

| | |
|---|---|
| *M.M.* | *The Mariner's Mirror* |
| *N.B.G.B.* | *Naval Biography of Great Britain*, by James Ralfe, 4 vols. (1828) |
| *N.M.* | *Nautical Magazine* |
| *N.M.M.* | National Maritime Museum, Greenwich |
| *U.S.J.* | *United Service Journal and Naval and Military Magazine* |
| O'Byrne | *O'Byrne Naval Biography* (1849) |
| *P.P.* | *Parliamentary Papers* |
| P.R.O. | Public Record Office, Kew, London |
| Tesler | Mario Tesler, *Malvinas: Como EE. UU. Provoco In Unsurpacion Inglesa* (1979) |
| Whitington | G.T. Whitington, *The Falklands Islands . . .* (1840) |

# Notes

## Chapter 1: Prologue: The Key to the Pacific

1. The Falkland Islands Dependencies have an aggregate land mass of one million square miles. They include South Georgia, South Sandwich Islands, the South Orkneys, South Shetlands and Graham Land – in a sector 20 to 80 degrees W., with the apex at the South Pole. They were annexed to the British Crown by Letters Patent of 1908 (amended in 1917).
2. John James Onslow, Remarks on the Falkland Islands and the Western Coast of Mexico (1833), Rb. 258, in Misc, Papers, vol. 59 (Ad 6), H.D.
3. Ibid.
4. Quoted in Julius Goebel, Jr., *The Struggle for the Falklands Islands: A Study in Legal and Diplomatic History* (New Haven: Yale University Press, 1927; reprint, 1982), p. 1.
5. Ibid.
6. Ibid.
7. *A.R.*, 1771, p. 2.
8. Glyndwr Williams, ' "The Inexhaustible Fountain of Gold": English Projects and Ventures in the South Seas, 1670–1750,' in John E. Flint and Glyndwr Williams, eds., *Prespectives of Empire: Essays Presented to Gerald S. Graham* (London: Longman, 1973), p. 29.
9. Ibid., pp. 28-30.
10. Ibid., p. 46.

11. Glyndwr Williams, ed., *Documents Relating to Anson's Voyage Round the World, 1740-44* (London: Navy Records Society, 1967) contains a complete explanation of these achievements.
12. Quoted in Williams, "Inexhaustible Fountain of Gold," p. 51.
13. Quoted, ibid., p. 52.
14. Ibid.
15. Instructions to the Hon. John Byron, Captain of His Maj's ship the *Dolphin*, 17 June 1764, Adm. 2/1332. Samuel Johnson, *Thoughts on the Late Transactions Respecting Falkland's Islands* (1771; new ed., Leigh-on-Sea, Essex: Thames Bank Publishing Co. Ltd., 1948), p. 13. Vincent T. Harlow, *The Founding of the Second British Empire, 1763-1793* (2 vols.: London: Longmans, Green and Co., 1952, 1964), 1: 3-4.
16. Robert E. Gallagher, ed., *Byron's Journal of His Circumnavigation* (Cambridge: Hakluyt Society, 2nd ser., no. 122, 1964), p. 60.
17. Account by Captain Mouat of H.M.S. *Tamar*; quoted in ibid.
18. The Rev. Richard Walter, *A Voyage Round the World* (London, 1769 ed.), pp. 126-27. Anson recommended a survey of the archipelago. See Glyndwr Williams, ed., *Documents Relating to Anson's Voyage Round the World, 1740-1744* (London: Navy Records Society, 1967), pp. 272-73.
19. Quoted in Boyson, p. 44. Byron to Earl of Egmont, sent via *Florida* storeship, 24 February 1765, Adm. 1/162; *Byron's Journal*, pp. 153-60.
20. Egmont to the Duke of Grafton, 20 July 1765, S.P. 94/253, P.R.O.: *Byron's Journal*, pp. 160-63. On Egmont, *D.N.B.*, 44 (1895): 379-73.
21. Copy of a Letter from Mr. Secretary (Henry) Conway (for the Southern Department) to The Lords of the Admiralty, 20 July 1765, in *F.I.J.*, 1975, pp. 21-23. Original in S.P. Spain, Supplement, 253, P.R.O.
22. *Byron's Journal*, pp. lxvi-lxvii. After Byron's return Egmont represented to the King (H.M.C. *Appendix to the VII Report* (MSS of Earl of Egmont) (1879), p. 232): 'that the knowledge

of the ports in the Falkland Islands and of the Straits of Magellan would greatly facilitate further discoveries in the Pacific Ocean south of the Line, if pursued before a war with France or Spain, or the jealousy of those two powers should oblige Great Britain to part with the possession of the Falkland Islands, or otherwise interrupt the attempts of Great Britain in that part of the world.'

23. McBride to the Earl of Egmont, 6 April 1766, copy, *F.I.J.*, 1976, p. 32. Secret instructions to Captain McBride, 26 September 1765, Adm. 2/1332, pp. 135-39.

24. Quoted in W.L. Allardyce, *The Story of the Falkland Islands: Being an Account of their Discovery and Early History, 1500-1842* (reprint, Letchworth, Herts.: Garden City Press, 1915), p. 21. McBride's report, 21 March 1767, Adm. 1/2116. Samuel Johnson adopted McBride's language liberally: '*Nil mortabilus arduum est*. There is nothing which human courage will not undertake, and little that human patience will not endure. The garrison lived upon Falkland's Island, shrinking from the blast, and shuddering at the billows.' Johnson, *Thoughts on the Late Transactions Respecting Falkland's Islands*, p. 15.

25. McBride to Commanding Officer of a Settlement in Berkeley's Sound, Falklands Island, 4 December 1766, Add MS. 32603, f. 36, B.L.

26. John Dunmore, *French Explorers in the Pacific, Volume I: The Eighteenth Century* (Oxford: Clarendon Press, 1965), pp. 57-69.

27. Here I have relied closely and extensively on the details as provided in Maurice Thiéry, *Bougainville, Soldier and Sailor*, trans. Anne Agnew (London: Grayson & Grayson, 1932), p. 121 ff. Bougainville's brief account of these proceedings is found in his *Voyage autour du monde par la fregate du Roi la Boudeuse et la flute L'Etoile en 1766-1769* (Paris, 1771). English translation by John Reinhold Forster, London, 1771, pp. 37 ff. See also A.J. Pernetty, *Histoire d'un Voyage aux iles Malouines fait en 1763 et 1764* (2 vols., Paris, 1770).

28. Thiéry, *Bougainville*, p. 122.

29. Ibid., pp. 123-24.

30. Quoted, ibid., pp. 130-31.

31. Ibid., p. 131.
32. Quoted, ibid., p. 132.
33. Ibid., p. 134.
34. Quoted, ibid., p. 137.
35. Dunmore, *French Explorers*, p. 62
36. Ibid., p. 63.
37. Ibid.
38. Ibid.
39. Thiéry, *Bougainville*, pp. 142–43.
40. Ibid., pp. 152–53.
41. On this Anglo-French interrelationship, see Boyson, *Falkland Islands*, pp. 46–50. Goebel dismisses McBride's conduct as 'highly irregular,' an overstatement (p. 240). *Correspondence of William Pitt, Earl of Chatham* (4 vols.; London: John Murray, 1838–40), 3:119.
42. Bougainville, *Memoire sur les Iles Maloines*, also Ossun to Choiseul, 28 April 1766, both in Archives des Affaires Etrangeres, Paris; cited in Allan Christlelow, 'Great Britain and the Trades from Cadiz and Lisbon to Spanish America and Brazil, 1759–1783,' *H.A.H.R.*, 28, 1 (February 1948), pt. 2, p. 26.
43. 'Account of the Island and Province of Chiloé. Extracted from the Remark Book kept on board H.M.S. *Pylades* by Captain Blanckley, R.N.,' *Journal of the Royal Geographical Society*, 4 (1834): 344–61.
44. John C. Beaglehole, *The Exploration of the Pacific* (3rd ed.; London: A. & C. Black, 1966), p. 181.
45. Paul Groussac, *Les Iles Malouines* (Buenos Aires: Anales de la Biblioteca Nacional, 1910), p. 538. Bucareli's instructions, 25 February 1768, in Goebel, pp. 271–72.
46. Viscount Weymouth to James Harris, 12 September 1770, and related correspondence, in *Papers Relative to the Late Negotiation with Spain*, p. 6 ff.
47. Ibid., pp. 31–33.
48. Allardyce, *Falkland Islands*, pp. 22–24. Nicholas Tracy, 'The Falkland Islands Crisis of 1770: Use of Naval Force,' *English Historical Review*, 90 (January 1975): 40–75. *Papers Relative to the Late Negotiation with Spain;* and *the Taking of Falkland's Island* (London: State Papers, 1777) contains the

main correspondence on this aspect of the dispute. See also *A.R.*, 1771. The diplomacy is retold in Goebel, pp. 302–409. A clearer explanation of the restitution is given in Boyson, p. 70 ff. Also Harlow, *Founding of the Second British Empire*, 1:31 and José Torré Revello, *La promesa secretary el convenio anglo-españo sombre les Malvinas de 1771 (neuvas aportaciones)*, (Buenos Aires: Imprenta de la Universidad, publicaciones del Investigaciones Histórucas, No, 98, 1952).

49. Bernard Penrose, *An Account of the Last Expedition to Port Egmont in Falkland's Island in the year 1772, Together with the Transactions of the Company of the Penguin Shallop During their Stay There* (London: J. Johnson, 1775); quoted in Allardyce, *Falkland Islands*, pp. 24–26.

50. This report began as Lieutenant S.W. Clayton, 'A Short Description of Falkland Islands, Their Produce, Climate and Natural History,' enclosed in Clayton to Phillip Stephens, 29 September 1774, Adm. 7/704. Printed with modifications, in *The Philosophical Transactions of the Royal Society*, 66 (1776): 99–108.

51. Quoted in Allardyce, *Falkland Islands*, pp. 26–27.

52. *The Gentlemen's Magazine*, 16 August 1774; also, Ann Shirley, 'H.M.S. *Endeavour* and the Falklands,' *M.M.*, 70, 1 (February 1984): 95–96.

53. B.L., Add. MS. 32603, fol. 6b; quoted in Boyson, p. 76.

54. Boyson, pp. 79–81. On threatened exile to the Falklands, see the case cited by Peggy K. Liss, *Atlantic Empires: The Network of Trade and Revolution, 1813-1826* (Baltimore: Johns Hopkins University Press, 1983), p. 291 n. 27.

55. Of Spain's subsequent destruction of the English site, the supercargo of the *Queen Charlotte* advised his reader: 'This affair made a great noise in London, and occasioned much clamour amongst the politicians of the time. . . . just observe, that we need not wonder at the Spaniards envying us the possession of these islands, as their situation commands the passage to the Spanish Settlements in the South Seas.' [William Beresford], *A Voyage Round the World, but more particularly to the North-West Coast. . . . 1785-1788* (London, 1789), p. 40.

56. Port Egmont, Captain Charles Hope of the *Tyne* noted in

December 1832, constituted 'a large and excellent harbour .
. . completely landlocked.' He continued: 'Although . . .
such a splendid Harbour, it is by no means easy for a stran-
ger to find it out, in very hazy weather, which was our case.
The puzzling thing is to be quite sure you round the proper
two small islands. . . .' (Remark book, *Tyne*, dated 4 January
1833, Misc. Papers 58 (Ad. 5ii), H.D.) Similar views were
held by Master Edward W. Gulliver of the *Tyne*, Misc.
Papers 58 (Ad.5i). See also, 'Remarks on the Falkland
Islands, visited by H.M.S. *Tyne*, Charles Hope, Esq.,
Captain, in January 1833, by Mr Edward Gulliver, Master,
R.N.,' *N.M.*, 3, 29 (July 1834): 387–89.

## Chapter 2: Trade, War and Revolution in the South Atlantic

1. See, for instance, Warren L. Cook, *Floodtide of Empire: Spain
   and the Pacific Northwest, 1543–1819* (New Haven: Yale
   University Press, 1973).
2. On Lord Anson's successful taking of the Manila Galleon,
   see Glyndwr Williams, ed., *Documents Relating to Anson's
   Voyage Round the World, 1740–1744* (London: Navy Records
   Society, 1967), pp. 3–44, 109–11 and 183–225.
3. J. Holland Rose, A.P. Newton, and E.A. Benians, eds., *Cambridge History of the British Empire*, vol. 2: *The New Empire,
   1783–1870* (Cambridge: Cambridge University Press,
   1961), p. 545.
4. Edmund Fanning, *Voyages Round the World* (New York:
   Collins and Hannay, 1833), pp. 84–97, 361–64 and 416.
   The standard work on the economic aspects is Antony B.
   Dickinson, 'Sealing in the Falkland Islands and Dependencies,' Ph. D. thesis, Cambridge University, 1987.
5. [Beresford], *Voyage Round the World*, p. 42.
6. *N.M.*, 3, 17 (July 1833): 395–98.
7. Entries for 4–22 January 1795, *Log of the Union: John Boit's
   Remarkable Voyage to the Northwest Coast and Around the World,
   1794–1796*, edited by Edmund Hayes (Portland: Oregon
   Historical Society, 1981), pp. 20–25. See also, Samuel E.
   Morison, *The Maritime History of Massachusetts 1783–1860*
   (Boston: Houghton Mifflin, 1961 printing), pp. 61 and 74.

8. James Grant, R.N., 'Extracts from *The Narrative of a Voyage of Discovery performed in H.M.'s Vessel* The Lady Nelson. . . . *1800, 1801 and 1802 to New South Wales* (London: C. Roworth, 1803),' *F.I.J.*, 1974, pp. 36–39.

9. As the case of the snow *Mercury* of New Providence, Rhode Island attests. See Michael Roe, ed., *The Journal and Letters of Captain Charles Bishop on the North-West Coast of America in the Pacific and in New South Wales 1794–1799* (Cambridge: Hakluyt Society, 2nd ser., no. 131, 1967), p. 94 and passim.

10. Morison, *Maritime History of Massachusetts*, p. 61.

11. See also Lachlan Bellingham Mackinnon, *Some Account of the Falkland Islands, From a Six Months' Residence in 1838 and 1839* (London: A.H. Baily and Co., 1840), p. 43.

12. Ibid., p. 42.

13. Fanning, *Voyages*, pp. 360–61.

14. Ibid., pp. 416–18. David E. Long, *Sailor–Diplomat: A Biography of Commodore James Biddle, 1783–1848* (Boston: Northeastern University Press, 1983), p. 63 ff.

15. A. Howard Clark, 'The Antarctic Fur Seal and Sea-Elephant Industry,' in George Brown Goode, ed., *The Fisheries and Fishery Industries of the United States* (Washington, D.C.: Government Printing Office, 1887), Section 5, Volume 2, part 18, no. 3, pp. 400–67. Ian Strange, 'Sealing Industries of the Falkland Islands,' *F.I.J.*, 1972, unpaginated issue.

16. Claims of Bristol Merchants, 1 June 1790, in T. Taylor to (Grenville or E. Nepean), 2 June 1790, Home Office Papers 42/16 (29), P.R.O. James Colnett, *A Voyage to the South Atlantic and Round Cape Horn into the Pacific Ocean* (London: 1798). Colnett's journal, 'A Voyage for Whaling and Discovery round Cape Horn . . . 1793 and 1794,' is in *B.L.*, Add. MS. 30/369. See, especially, ff. 255–56. This theme is ably developed in D. Mackay, *In the Wake of Cook* (New York: St. Martins, 1980).

17. Charles Haskins Townsend, 'Where the Nineteenth Century Whaler Made His Catch,' *Bulletin of the New York Zoological Society*, 34, 6 (November–December 1931): 173–9.

18. Clayton, 'Account of Falkland Islands,' p. 108n.

19. Quoted in Destéfani, *The Malvinas*, pp. 77–78. James Weddell, Master R.N., *A Voyage Towards the South Pole . . .*

*1822–24* (London: Longman 1825). A similar view was held by Fanning (*Voyages*, p. 273).

20. Fanning, *Voyages*, p. 421

21. Edouard A. Stackpole, *Whales and Destiny; The Rivalry between America, France and Britain for Control of the Southern Whale Fishery, 1705–1825* (Amherst: University of Massachusetts Press, 1972), esp. pp. 115–25, 146–57, and 262–66. Also, Harry S. Morton, *The Whale's Wake* (Honolulu: University of Hawaii Press, 1982) and Gordon Jackson, *The British Whaling Trade* (London: A. & C. Black, 1978).

22. Captain James Hillyar to J.W. Croker, 30 March 1814, Valparaiso Bay, encl. in Rear-Admiral Sir Manley Dixon to Croker, 10 June 1814, Adm. 1/22.

23. *Historical Records of Australia*, ser. 1, vol. 8 (1916): 75–76 and 654. Also, Down, p. 90.

24. Rudy Bauss, 'Rio de Janeiro: Strategic Base for the Global Designs of the British Royal Navy, 1777–1815,' in Craig L. Symonds et al., *New Aspects of Naval History* (Annapolis Md.: Naval Institute Press, 1981), pp. 75–89.

25. Duke of Clarence to Otway, 19 February 1826, in *N.B.G.B.*, 4:23; also *D.N.B.*, 42 (1895):347 and O'Byrne, pp. 841–44.

26. Basil Hall, *Extracts from a Journal, Written on the Coasts of Chile, Peru, and Mexico in the Years 1820, 1821, 1822* (2 vols.: Edinburgh: Archibald Constable & Co., 1824), 1:42; also Gerald S. Graham and R. Humphreys, eds., *The Navy and South America, 1807–1823: Correspondence of the Commanders in Chief on the South American Station* (London: Navy Records Society, vol. 104, 1962), p. xi. Further particulars may be found in Barry M. Gough, 'Sea Power and South America: The Royal Navy's "Brazils" or South American Station, 1808–1837,' *The American Neptune*, 50, 1 (1990): 26–34.

27. Alan K. Manchester, *British Preeminence in Brazil: Its Rise and Decline* (Chapel Hill, N.C.: University of North Carolina Press, 1933) and Graham and Humphreys, *Navy and South America*, pp. xxv–xxvi.

28. Rear-Admiral Sir Manley Dixon to J.W. Croker, 20 April 1814, No. 156, Adm. 1/22; also Bowles to Dixon, 11 April 1814, encl. in Dixon to Croker, 16 April 1814, No. 152, ibid.

29. Graham and Humphreys, eds., *Navy and South America*, p. xxxiv.

30. Charles R. Boxer, *The Dutch Seaborne Empire, 1600–1800* (London: Hutchinson, 1966; new printing 1977), pp. 242–67.

31. Commodore J.Blankett to Evan Nepean, 25 January 1795, in W.G. Perrin, ed., *The Keith Papers, Vol. 1* (London: Navy Records Society, vol. 62, 1927), p.214.

32. Gerald S. Graham, *Great Britain in the Indian Ocean: A Study of Maritime Enterprise, 1800–50* (Oxford: Clarendon Press, 1967), p.24.

33. Sir John Barrow, *Autobiographical Memoir* (London: John Murray 1847), p. 252, and, by the same, *An Account of Travels into . . . Southern Africa . . .* (2 vols.: London: T. Cadell & W. Davies, 1801, 1804), 2:305. See also Judith Blow Williams, *British Commercial Policy and Trade Expansion, 1750–1815* (Oxford: Clarendon Press, 1972), p. 32.

34. Sir John W. Fortescue, *A History of the British Army, Vol. 5 (1803–1807)* (London: Macmillan, 1910), pp. 310–18 and 369–437. I am also indebted to the unpublished paper 'An Account of the British Expedition to the River Plate in 1806 and 1807' (1979) with Addendum (1983), both deposited in the Scott Polar Research Institute, Cambridge.

35. *D.N.B.*, 156 (1897): 143–46. Popham had only recently been cleared of charges of extraordinary expenditures on repairs to H.M.S. *Romney*, his vindication coming at the hands of a parliamentary committee. On his imperial schemes for a marine establishment in eastern seas, see his *A Description of Prince of Wales Island, in the Streights of Malacca . . .* (London: J. Stockdale, 1805), p. 35, and Williams, *British Commercial Policy*, p. 80.

36. Liss, *Atlantic Empires*, p. 188.

37. 'Miranda and the British Admiralty, 1804–1806,' *American Historical Review*, 6 (1901): 508–30. C.F. Mullett, ed., 'British Schemes and Spanish America in 1806,' *H.A.H.R.*, 27 (1947): 269–78, Popham had wanted to serve with Miranda in 1803 in the wars of South American independence. Miranda said he 'thought like an Englishman' in regards to the continent, that is, he wanted English markets

in South America. William S. Robertson, *The Life of Miranda* (2 vols.: Chapel Hill, N.C.: University of North Carolina Press, 1929), 1: 257–58, 260, 275–77 and 322–23.

38. *Trial of Sir Home Popham . . . 1807* (London: John Fairburn, 1807); *D.N.B.*, 46; (1896): 145–46; *D.N.B.*, 61 (1900): 120–21. Ione S. Wright and Lisa M. Nekhom, *Historical Dictionary of Argentina* (Metuchen, N.J. & London: Scarecrow Press, 1978), pp. 86–87. Bartolome Mitre's *Historia de Belgrano y de la Independencia Argentine* (4th ed.; 3 vols., 1887) is the definitive introduction to the revolutionary struggle.

39. Witness these telling instructions from the Secretary of State of Beresford, 21 September 1806: "We have for long been restrained from invading Spanish South America by the fear of exciting a revolt against Spain, which could only be controlled by a British force of superior strength. It is with this view, as much as with that of securing valuable possesions that your force has been so much increased. Use your judgement and your troops principally to avert the evil of such a revolt as we have mentioned, making none but unavoidable changes in the Government." (Quoted in Fortescue, *History of the Army*, 5: 374).

40. Fortescue, *History of the Army*, 5: 376; also Robert Craufurd, *An Authentic Narrative of the proceedings of the Expedition under the Command of Brigadier-General Craufurd . . .* (London: printed for the author, 1808).

41. Ibid, p. 436.

42. D.C.M. Platt, *Finance, Trade, and Politics in British Foreign Policy, 1815–1914* (Oxford: Clarendon Press, 1968), p. 312.

43. Harold Temperley, *The Foreign Policy of Canning, 1822–1827* (London: G. Bell Sons, 1925), pp. 184–85.

44. See Salisbury's Mansion House speech of July 1897, quoted in Henry S. Ferns, *Britain and Argentina in the Nineteenth Century* (Oxford Clarendon Press, 1960), p. 465. Platt, *Finance, Trade, and Politics*, p. 322–23. John F. Cady, *Foreign Intervention in the Rio de la Plata 1838–50; A Study of French, British and American Policy in Relation to the Dictator Juan Manuel Rosas* (Philadelphia: University of Pennsylvania Press, 1929).

45. As Vice-Admiral the Hon. Michael De Courcy did in regard

to royalists blockading Montevideo. See his letter to Blio, 7 September 1811, F.O. 63/103; see also Williams, *British Commercial Policy*, p. 256. For a different case, in 1817, when a British naval captain insisted that a Portugese blockade should not exclude the British from their usual business, see Chamberlain to Castlereagh, 25 January 1819, F.O. 63/220; also, Williams, *British Commercial Policy*, p. 265.

46. Ibid., p. 189, E.J.Pratt, 'Anglo-American Commercial and Political Rivalry on the Plata, 1820–1830,' *H.A.H.R.*, 113 (August 1931): 302–35. See also, J. Kellenbenz, 'German Shipowners on the Transatlantic Routes: The Case of Brazil and the Rio de la Plata, 1815–1850', paper presented to Shipowner in History Symposium, National Maritime Museum, Greenwich, September 1984. Sir Charles K. Webster, *Britain and the Independence of Latin America* (2 vols.; London: Oxford University Press, 1938), 1:13; also, Williams, *British Commercial Policy*, p. 257.

47. Rear-Admiral Sir William Sidney Smith to the Hon. W.W. Pole, 24 February 1809, Adm. 1/19.

48. John Lynch, *Argentina Dictator: Juan Manuel de Rosas, 1829–1852* (Oxford: Clarendon Press, 1981).

49. John Street, 'Lord Strangford and the Rio de la Plata, 1808–1815,' *H.A.H.R.*, 33 (1953): 481. Also, Leslie Bethell, 'The Independence of Brazil and the Abolition of the Brazilian Slave Trade: Anglo-Brazilian Relations, 1822–1826,' *Journal of Latin American Studies*, 1 (1969): 115–47, *D.N.B.*, 46 (1896): pp. 86–87.

50. A concise account of British policy in regards to the Brazil–Argentine War, and based on the F.O. 6 correspondence, is to be found in Ferns, *Britain and Argentina*, ch. VI. *D.N.B.*, 43 (1895): 213–14. Obituary in *Proceedings, Royal Geographical Society*, new ser., 4 (10 October 1882): 612–13. Nina Louisa Key Shuttleworth, *A Life of Sir Woodbine Parish, K.C.H., F.R.S., 1796–1882* (London: Smith, Elder & Co., 1910). Parish to Canning, 30 July 1824, No. 43, enclosing Report on the Trade of the R. Plate, F.O. 6/4.

51. Parish's reports or communications relating to South America and the Falkland Islands are in the *Journal of the Royal Geographical Society*, 3 (1833): 94–105, 4, pt. 2 (1834):

182–91, 7 (1837): 381–87, and 31 (1841): 204–7. His rich collection of Buenos Aires documents, 1766–1830, is in the B.L., Add. MSS. 32603–9.

52. *D.N.B.*, vol. 42 (1895): 364. A hostile account of his mission to the Rio de la Plata was republished in 1847 from *La Gaceta Mercantil*, the organ of Rosas (ibid.).

53. 'Statement of Shipping . . . 1832,' *N.M.*, 1833, p. 515. The history of British hydrography in these seas awaits a scholar. However, for an introduction see George Basalla, 'The Beagle Voyage without Darwin,' *M.M.*, 49, 1 (1963) and G.S. Ritchie, *The Admiralty Chart: British Naval Hydrography in the Nineteenth Century* (London: Hollis and Carter, 1967), ch. 12.

54. Webster, *Britain and Latin America*, 1:11. Bolivar quoted in Dexter Perkins, *The Monroe Doctrine, 1823–26* (Cambridge, Mass.,: Harvard University Press, 1932), p. 154. Also, Desmond C.M. Platt, *Business Imperialism, An Inquiry based on British Experience in Latin America (1808–1830)* (Baltimore: Johns Hopkins University Press, 1969), pp. 303–15.

55. Memorandum of a conference between Polignac and Canning, 8–12 October 1823, encl. in Canning to Stuart, 9 November 1823, F.O. 146/56, P.R.O. (printed in Harold Temperley and Lillian Penson, eds., *Foundations of British Foreign Policy: Documents Old and New from Pitt to Salisbury* (Cambridge: Cambridge University Press, 1938), pp. 70–76. Also, *B.F.S.P.*, vol. 11, pp. 49–53.

56. Dexter Perkins, *The United States and Latin America* (Baton Rouge, La.: Louisiana State University Press, 1961), pp. 16–17, and J. Fred. Rippy, *Rivalry of the United States and Great Britain over Latin America (1808–1830)* (Baltimore: John Hopkins University Press, 1929), pp. 303–15.

57. *D.N.B.*, vol. 20 (1889): 128–29. Cf. Temperley, *Foreign Policy of Canning*, p. 266.

## Chapter 3: Britannia Triumphant, and the Argentine Rival

1. Admiral Sir Cyprian Bridge, *Sea-Power and Otter Studies* (London: Smith, Elder & Co., 1910), pp. 63–64.

2. *Hansard*, 1st ser., 32: 1104.

3. Sir Halford J. Mackinder, *Democratic Ideas and Reality* (London Constable & Co., 1919), p. 73. Albert H. Imlah, *Economic Elements in the 'Pax Britannica'* (Cambridge, Mass.: Harvard University Press, 1958), p. 186. Gerald S. Graham, *'Peculiar Interlude: The Expansion of England in a Period of Peace, 1815–1850'* (George Arnold Wood Memorial Lecture, University of Sidney, 1959) and by the same author, *The Politics of Naval Supremacy* (Cambridge: Cambridge University Press, 1965), ch. 4. See also, Christopher J. Bartlett, *Great Britain and Sea Power, 1815–1853* (Oxford: Clarendon Press, 1963), a valuable study of the internal politics of the British government facing a series of threats to their naval supremacy which was sometimes more illusory than real.

4. Most of the larger islands of the South Atlantic, including Gough Island, a dependency of Tristan da Cunha, were unsettled (save for a castaway or adventurer) at the time of their acquisition. Tristan da Cunha was occupied only for political reasons; but the garrison was withdrawn in 1817 when the sometime military governor, Rear-Admiral Sir George Cockburn, advised Viscount Melville, First Lord of the Admiralty, that unlike Ascension which lay on the same trade wind with St. Helena, and a small vessel might run down to it from St. Helena in three or four days with the greatest ease, Tristan da Cunha lay twenty degrees south of Napoleon's jail and that, in consequence, rescue missions could as easily be launched from the West African coast or from Europe or America. The garrison was consequently withdrawn to the Cape in November 1817. J. Brander, *Tristan da Cunha, 1506–1902* (London: George Allen & Urwin, 1940), pp. 63–94. American activities in and near Tristan da Cunha are described in N.M. Wace, 'The Discovery, Exploitation and Settlement of the Tristan da Cunha,' *Islands Proceedings, Royal Geographical Society of Australia, South Australian Branch*, 70 (1969): 11–40.

5. Much has been written on the aims and objectives of British "imperialism" in the nineteenth century but none so clearly reasoned as that of Professor Platt in his *Finance, Trade, and Politics in British Foreign Policy*, esp. p. 367. See also the discussion here in Chapter 7.

6. Goebel, p. 423. Boyson wryly calls this a modest assumption (p. 82).

7. Remark Book, H.M.S. *Rinaldo*, 1 July 30 November 1824, Misc. Papers, vol. 50 (Ad.2), p. 678, H.D.

8. M. Camille de Roquefeuil, *A Voyage Round the World, Between the Years 1816–1819* (London: Phillips, 1823; Phillips' Voyages, vol. 9). pp. 4–5.

9. Robert FitzRoy, *Narrative of the Surveying Voyages of His Majesty's Ships Adventure and Beagle, Between the Years 1826 and 1836.* Vol. 2, *Proceedings of the Second Expedition, 1831–1836, Under the Command of Captain Robert FitzRoy* (London: H. Colburn, 1839), p. 236. An appendix to this volume, containing some Falklands material (pp. 149–62), was published simultaneously.

10. See [Charles H. Barnard], *A Narrative of the Sufferings and Adventures of Captain Charles H. Barnard, in A Voyage Round the World. . . . 1812–1816; embracing an account of the seizure of his vessel at the Falkland Islands, by an English crew whom he had rescued from the horrors of a shipwreck (etc.)* (New York: J. Lindon, 1829). Republished as *Marooned*, Bertha S. Dodge, ed. (Middletown, Ct.: Wesleyan University Press, 1979). Details at p. 42.

10. Boyson, pp. 88–89. The *Pierre Lovit*, a French ship, was lost in Falkland Sound in 1833, the *Frances*, a whaling brig of London, was wrecked on New Island in 1842, and John Smith's 1977 *Plan of the Falkland Islands* shows upwards of a hundred others.

11. Gabriel Franchère, *Journal of a Voyage to the North West Coast, 1811–14* (Toronto: The Champlain Society, 1969).

12. The *Salem Gazette* of 8 June 1821 printed Jewitt's circular letter received by Captain W.B. Orne of the Salem schooner *General Knox*, returned from the Falklands. Reproduced in *B.F.S.P.*, 20: 422n. The substance of it was published in the *Cadiz Redactor* August 1821. Paul Groussac, *Las Islas Malvinas* (1909; Buenos Aires: Comision Protectora de Bibliotecas Populares, 1936), p. 24, n. 16.

13. Alvear to Forsyth, 21 March 1839, Washington, D.C., in Manning, pp. 222–23.

14. Robert Greenhow, 'The Falkland Islands,' *Hunt's Merchants'*

*Magazine* (New York), 6, 2 (February 1842): 134. The best biographical data on Jewitt, explaining the confusing details, is Tessler, note beginning p. 37 and ending p. 41. Also, Destéfani, *The Malvinas*, p. 77.

15. James Weddell, Master R.N., *A Voyage Towards the South Pole, 1822-24* (London: Longman, Hunt, Rees, Orme, Brown and Green, 1825), pp. 103-12.

16. Ibid., p. 106.

17. Ibid., p. 112.

18. Jewitt to Weddell, 2 November 1820, Puerto Soledad, in ibid., p.104.

19. These and following particulars are from what might be termed the official history of Argentine occupation of the Falklands 1820-32, more correctly, *Report of the Political and Military Commandant of the Malvinas*, by Louis Vernet, translation, *B.F.S.P.*, vol. 20.

20. Ibid., p. 419.

21. Decree of 22 October 1821: Fishery on the Pantagonian Coast, translation in ibid., p. 421.

22. Report of the Political and Military Commandant, *B.F.S.P.*, 20: 419.

23. Biographical particulars can be found in Wright and Neckholme, *Historical Dictionary of Argentina*, pp. 1007-1008.

24. Letter of an officer, R.N., to FitzRoy quoted in FitzRoy, *Narrative*, 2: 266. Among his strongest admirers was Woodbine Parish who arranged to have Vernet's report on the productions and climate of the Falklands published in the *Journal of the Royal Geographical Society*, 3 (1833): 94-105. This paper, 'Account of East Falkland Island,' was read to the Society on 14 January 1833 within a fortnight of the *Clio's* act of reoccupation.

25. Advertisement and Directions by William Low, 2 September 1831, Montevideo, forwarded from J.W. Walker, Liverpool, with two tracings (30 January 1832), in Misc. Papers 58 (Ad. 5 (ii)), pp. 381-84, H.D.

26. Report of the Political and Military Commandant, *B.F.S.P.*, 20: 419.

27. Allardyce, *Falkland Islands*, p. 30. 'There is a settlement here

from Buenos Ayres who supply shipping with very good cattle which they kill in the mountains where there are abundance, the old ones killed for their hides and tallow but young ones are borught down and kept on Goat Island. There are also wild Ducks, Hogs, Geese, Rabbits and in fact every species of waterfowl in abundance. Those are killed in or near the small lakes of fresh water to which the Island abound.' Remarks of H.M.S. *Tribune*, Capt. John Wilson, Misc. Papers, 58 (Ad. 5 (ii)), H.D.

28. *B.F.S.P.*, 20: 425.
29. Destéfani, *The Malvinas*, pp. 80–81.
30. Ibid., p. 81.
31. *B.F.S.P.*, 20: 423. José Luis Muñoz Azpiri et al., *Historia Completa de Las Malvinas* (3 vols.: Buenos Aires: Oriente, 1966), 2: 63–4 and 3: 11.
32. Report on the Political and Military Commandant, *B.F.S.P.*, 20: 430.
33. Parish to the Earl of Aberdeen, 15 March 1829, No. 17, F.O. 6/499.
34. Ibid. Parish to Aberdeen, 25 April 1829, no. 24, ibid.: also Down, p. 107. Shuttleworth, *Parish*, pp. 359-60.
35. Beckington to Sir Robert Peel, 11 July 1829, F.O. 6/499.
36. Quoted in Down, pp. 103-104. Also, Otway to John Wilson Croker, 2 April 1829, no. 28, Adm. 1/31, Qa76.
37. Langdon to T.P. Macqueen, 12 April 1829, C.O. 78/1. On Langdon, see O'Byrne, p. 630.
38. Memorandum on the Falkland Islands (10 July 1829), in circular letter of 12 July 1829, C.O. 78/2. The Memorandum is reproduced in Down, App. A.
39. The Duke of Wellington to Sir George Murray (Secretary of State for War and the Colonies), 25 July 1829, in *Despatches, Correspondence, and Memoranda of Field Marshal Arthur Duke of Wellington*, K.G., vol. 6 (London: John Murray, 1877), pp. 41, 48-49.
40. Ibid.
41. Ibid.
42. John Barrow to Robert Hay (C.O.), 2 July 1829, C.O. 303/146, pp. 95-96.
43. Vattel, *Law of Nations* (Dublin, 1787 ed.), p. 163ff.

44. John Backhouse to Hay, 5 June 1829, C.O. 78/1. Murray to Wellington in *Despatches*, 6:41.
45. Bartlett, *Great Britain and Sea Power*, p. 60.
46. The Foreign Office solicited the opinion of the King's Advocate Herbert Jenner, King's Advocate to the Earl of Aberdeen, 28 July 1829, No. 40, F.O. 83/2227, pp. 102–105.
47. Draft of Official Note to be presented by Mr Parish, F.O. 6/27, fol. 16. Aberdeen to Parish, 8 August 1829, No. 5., F.O. 118/22, f. 197 (also F.O. 6/499). Shuttleworth, *Parish*, p. 360. Aberdeen's warm appreciation of Consul Parish is stated in his letter to Lord Holland, 28 October 1829, and his letter to Parish, 20 January 1830, Aberdeen Papers, Add. MSS 43234, fols. 41–41b and fol. 200 respectively, B.L. Also, Muriel E. Chamberlain, *Lord Aberdeen: A Political Biography* (London: Longman, 1983), pp. 246–47.
48. Parish to T. Guido, 19 November 1829, *B.F.S.P.*, 20: 346. Also, Parish to Aberdeen, 14 November 1829, No. 48, and Guido to Parish, 25 November 1829, F.O. 6/499.
49. Jenner to Aberdeen, 28 July 1829, No. 40, F.O. 83/2227, pp. 104–105.

### Chapter 4: The Eagle's Visitation

1. Deputation by Gilbert R. Davison, 23 November 1831, encl. in Slacum to Edward Livingston (U.S. Secretary of State), 23 November 1831, Buenos Aires, in Manning, pp. 66–68.
2. Slacum to Anchorena, ibid., p. 65.
3. Anchorena to Slacum, 25 November, and Slacum to Anchorena, 26 November 1831, ibid., pp. 70–71.
4. Paul D. Dickens, 'The Falkland Islands Dispute between the United States and Argentina,' *H.A.H.R.*, 9, 4 (November, 1929): 475. This article is a short, valuable critique of the episode (pp. 471–87). Further research could be undertaken in the materials on these three sealing vessels held in the mss. library, Mystic Seaport, Mystic, Conn., including the journal of the *Harriet*, letters regarding the arrest and detention of the *Breakwater*, and the account book of the *Superior*.

5. Anchorena to Slacum, 3 December 1831, Manning. p. 72.

6. Moore, p. 887.

7. By virtue of the prevalence of this practice this is not a matter of as great a moment as Boyson (p. 95) makes out: 'It is difficult to define why this young man's zeal for the honour of his country should make him sail under the flag of another nation.'

8. Down, p. 122.

9. *B.F.S.P.*, 20: 358-64. Dickens, 'Falkland Islands Dispute,' p. 476.

10. These letters and depositions are enclosed in Duncan to Slacum, 2 February 1832, Montevideo, in Manning, pp. 93-98.

11. Quoted in Dickens, 'Falkland Islands Dispute,' p. 477.

12. Martin Van Buren to John M. Forbes, 10 February 1831, Washington, in Manning, pp. 3-4.

13. Livingston to Francis Baylies, Consul, 14 December 1832, Washington, in Manning, p. 13.

14. Livingston to Baylies, 3 April 1832, Washington, ibid., p. 14.

15. Ibid.

16. A good scholar, Baylies wrote *An Historical Memoir of the Colony of New Plymouth* (1830), the enlarged (1866) edition of which contains a biographical sketch by S.G. Drake.

17. Livingston to Baylies, 26 January 1832, in Moore, p. 876.

18. Baylies to Maza, 20 June 1832, and Note of 10 July 1832, in *B.F.S.P.*, 20: 330-36, 338-40, and 350-52.

19. A very critical position for the aggressive, insensitive position of President Jackson is taken in Harold F. Peterson, *Argentina and the United States, 1810-1960* (New York: State University of New York, 1964), pp. 108-112.

20. Adams, *Memoirs*, 9: 446-47, quoted in Peterson, *Argentina and the United States*, p. 108.

21. Baylies to Livingston, 19 August 1832, in Manning, pp. 153-54.

22. Peterson, *Argentina and the United States*, pp. 112-13.

23. He had succeeded Woodbine Parish and in fact was first British minister plenipotentiary and envoy extraordinary to Buenos Aires. He moved to Rio in 1832 and to Washington

1835. He did much to ease Anglo-American feelings leading to the Webster–Ashburton treaty. *D.N.B.*, 20 (1889): 128–29.

24. Fox to Palmerston, 31 May 1832, no. 7, F.O. 118/26. He was not unsympathetic about American views on Vernet's piracy.
25. Ferns, *Britain and Argentina*, p. 230.
26. Fox to Palmerston, 15 October 1832, no. 17, F.O. 6/500.
27. Hood to Cox, 4 February 1832, encl. in Hood to Palmerston, 18 February 1832, No. 4, Montevideo, F.O. 51/8. Baker to Elliot, 10 July 1832, extract sent to Foreign Office 5 September 1832, copy, F.O. 6/499. Weddell, *Voyage* (1827 ed.), pp. 212 and 216; also, Down, pp. 96, 158, 161–162.
28. Graham to Palmerston, 22 March 1832, GC/CR/16, Broadlands MSS.
29. Dorothy K. Coveney and W.N. Medlicott, comps., *The Lion's Tail: An Anthology of Criticism and Abuse* (London: Constable, 1971), p. 19.
30. Baker to Elliot, 16 March 1832, and Adm. minute of 7 May 1832, Adm. 1/38.
31. Barrow to Hay, 4 August 1832, C.O. 78/1. Elliot to Sir George Shee (F.O.), 7 August 1832, F.O. 6/499.
32. Palmerston to Admiralty, 30 August 1832, Adm. 1/4249. Also, Admiralty to Foreign Office, 31 August 1832, F.O. 6/499.
33. The original of this celebrated despatch, 4 September 1832, is in F.O. 128/14. Gore's complaint of his difficult position, dated 17 January 1833 and addressed to Palmerston, is in F.O. 6/500, no. 4.

## Chapter 5: The Trident Strikes

1. Instructions to John James Onslow, 28 November 1832, copy, encl. in Baker to Elliot, 30 November 1832, Adm. 1/40; also in CapO, Adm. 1/1176 and Whittington, pp. 12–13.
2. Ibid.

3. He distinguished himself as second in command at Camperdown, 1797, was created a baronet, and given the freedom of the City of London. R.D. Franks, 'Admiral Sir Richard Onslow', *M.M.*, 67, 4 (November 1981): 327–337. *D.N.B.*, XLII: 225, *N.B.G.B.*, I: 350–53. Rear-Admiral C.B.H. Ross to J.J. Onslow, 12 April 1839, encl. in Onslow to Francis Beaufort, 3 October 1839, O.222, H.D.

4. These and other particulars on J.J. Onslow's life may be found in O'Byrne, p. 838, and John Marshall, *Royal Naval Biography*, vol. 4, pt. 2 (London: 1835), pp. 531–32.

5. Barry M. Gough, 'Specie Conveyance from the West Coast of Mexico in British Warships c. 1820–1870: An Aspect of the *Pax Britannica,*' *M.M.*, 69, 4 (November 1983): 419–33.

8. This amount he augmented rather handsomely a decade and a half later when he again went to the Pacific, this time in command of the sloop-of-war *Daphne*, and again came home with a hefty freight. Such reumuneration – 'one of the little pickings of the Pacific', as one officer put it rather wryly – was some certain compensation for a long wait on half pay. Ibid., pp. 426 and 432, n. 36. On the second freight conveyance Onslow was 'bumped' in seniority by the greedy the Hon. John Gordon of H.M.S. *America* who was courtmartialled and chastised for placing pecuniary ahead of national interests during the Oregon Crisis with the United States. Onslow had to wait his turn, and came home with a rich frieght from Guaymas, San Blas and Mazatlan. Barry M. Gough, 'H.M.S. *America* on the North Pacific Coast,' *Oregon Historical Quarterly*, 70, 4 (December 1969): 292–311. Commander F.M. Norman, *'Martello Tower' in China and the Pacific in Tribune* (London: George Allen, 1902), p. 59.

7. O'Byrne, p. 536.

8. By the time the *Tyne* completed her commission in January 1834, she had passed over 82,000 miles, a greater distance than had been transversed by any vessel since the Napoleonic Wars ended in 1815 (ibid.).

9. On Baker, see O'Byrne, p. 40. *N.B.G.B.*, 4: 237–55. He was Commander-in-Chief, South America, 6 March 1829–3; made K.C.B. 8 January 1831.

10. Instructions from Sir Thomas Baker, Rear Admiral of the

Red and Commander in Chief of H.M.'s ships and vessels employed on the South American Station to John James Onslow, Esq. (Commander of Sloop *Clio*), 28 November 1832, copy encl. in Baker to the Hon. G. Elliot, 30 November 1832, Adm. 1/40.

11. The original sources for this account of the Anglo-Argentine confrontation are: Onslow to Rear-Admiral Baker, 19 January 1833, Montevideo (reprinted in Whitington, pp. 15–18) and the fuller Onslow to Philip Yorke Gore, 19 January 1833, copies in Adm. 1/2276, and on the Argentine side, a report of Pinedo's proceedings and account, in Juan Ramon Balcarge and Manuel Vincente de Maza, 24 January 1833, Buenos Aires, *A.R.*, 1833, pp. 371–74. Also Onslow's Log, Adm. 51/3117–8, and Ship's Log, Adm. 53/258.

12. Boyson, p. 97. Whitington, p. 16. Pinedo's brief biography is an *Nuevo Diccionario Biografico Argentino*, 5 (1978): 504–505.

13. For sources, see n. 11, this chapter.

14. J.J. Onslow to His Excellency, the Commander of the Buenos Ayrean force at Port Luiz, Berkeley Sound, 2 January 1833, *A.R.*, 1833, p. 374.

15. Sources as in n. 3, this chapter.

16. Onslow to Baker and Onslow to Gore, both 19 January 1833, Adm. 1/2276.

17. O'Byrne, p. 838, *U.S.J.*, March 1833, p. 441 and July 1833, p. 389. Letters from Onslow to Elliot and Beaufort in O. 217, 218 and 219. H.D. Also, Charles J. Palmer, *The Perlustration of Great Yarmouth* (3 vols.: Great Yarmouth: George Nall, 1872–75), 3: 200.

18. *A.R.*, 1833, pp. 371–74.

19. Maza to Gore, 16 January, and Gore to Maza, 17 January 1833, in *A.R.*, 1833, pp. 374–5.

20. Gore to Palmerston, 14 February 1833, no. 5, F.O. 6/500.

21. Moreno to Palmerston, 24 April 1833, ibid.

22. Palmerston to Moreno, 27 April 1833, p. 308.

23. Moreno to Palmerston, 17 June 1833, F.O. 6/500 (trans. in *B.F.S.P.*, 23: 1366).

24. Palmerston to Moreno, 8 January 1834, F.O. 6/501; also

*B.F.S.P.*, 23: 1384–94. Goebel, pp. 457–58. Jenner to Palmerston, 30 November 1833, no. 53, F.O. 83/2227, p. 160.

25. Moreno to Aberdeen, 18 December, and Aberdeen to Moreno, 29 December 1841, *B.F.S.P.*, 31: 1003–1005. Moreno to Aberdeen, 8 March 1842. F.O. 6/502.

26. Gore to Rear-Admiral Sir M. Seymour, 27 June 1833, draft, in F.O. 118/31. Gore to Palmerston, 29 August 1834, no. 15, F.O. 6/501. Charles J. Hamilton to Palmerston, 19 October 1834, no. 3, F.O. 119/5.

27. *A.R.*, 1833, pp. 308–309.

## Chapter 6: John Bull's Isles

1. FitzRoy has his detractors, but his clear-thinking capacities ought not to be confused by critics of his Tory persuasions. His description is in the *Narrative of the Surveying Voyages . . . of Adventure and Beagle*, 2: 269 ff.

2. Nora Barlow, ed., *Charles Darwin's Diary of the Voyage of H.M.S. 'Beagle'* (Cambridge: Cambridge University Press, 1934), p. 138.

3. Onslow to Gore, 19 January 1833, Adm. 1/2276.

4. He had prepared an advertisement of supplies available to mariners, and sailing directions. J.W. Walker of Liverpool sent a copy to the Admiralty on 30 January 1832 (Misc. Papers, 58 (Ad. 5 (ii)), pp. 381–84, H.D. Charles Darwin's report on Low, this 'notorious and singular man' *(Diary*, p. 141), indicates that he was the 'terror' of those seas.

5. I do not suppose there is an inhabited civilized place where they are not to be found,' he added *(Diary*, p. 139).

6. Quoted in Richard Grove, 'Charles Darwin and the Falkland Islands,' *Polar Record*, 22, 139 (January 1985): 418.

7. Whitington, p. 22. *N.M.*, 3, 28 (1834), 376–77, containing Henry Rea's 18 November 1833 report and correcting the earlier 3, 25 (1834): 181. On Rea's assignment, see 'Recent Discoveries in the Antarctic Ocean,' *Journal of the Royal Geographical Society*, 3 (1833): 105–112.

8. *N.M.*, 3, 28 (1834): 377.

9. Boyson, p. 101. Other particulars from *N.M.*, 3, 29, pp. 436–38. On Gaucho Rivero see Captain Ernesto Manuel Campos, 'La Rebelion del Gaucho Antonio Rivero,' in Azpiri et al., *Historia Completa*, 3: 49–51, but more especially Juan Lucio Almeida, *Que Hizo El Gaucho Rivero en La Malvinas* (Buenos Aires: Plus Utra, Coleccion Esquemas Historicos, Vol. 8, 1972). See also, Richard Ware, 'The Case of Antonio Rivero and Sovereignty over the Falkland Islands,' *H.R.*, 27, 4 (1984): 961–67, and further discussion in the same periodical at 29, 2 (1986): 427–32 and 30, 3 (1987): 735–36.

10. Captain Charles Hope to Secretary of the Admiralty, 21 January 1833, and Hope to the Rt. Hon. James Townshend, Senior Officer, Pacific, 14 February 1833, both in Adm. 1/41, Qa 61.

11. Down, p. 148.

12. Darwin, *Diary*, p. 216. Rear-Admiral Sir Michael Seymouth, Bart., Instructions of December 1833 to Lieutenant Smith, quoted in John Skelly, 'The Falklands Story,' *F.I.J.*, 1984, p. 4 O'Byrne, p. 1086.

13. Skelly, 'Falklands Story,' pp. 8–9. Also Whitington, p. 23.

14. Hamond Journal, 3 September 1835, HAM/125, pp. 195–96, N.M.M.

15. Hamond Journal, 10 December 1834 and 1 January 1835, HAM/125, pp. 41, 50, N.M.M.

16. Some of the ships were the *Actaeon, Talbot, Blonde, North Star, Basilisk, Cleopatra*, and *Samarang*, besides several smaller vessels sent on particular assignment to the Falklands, the *Rapid, Sparrow, Snake*, and *Arrow* – all in the years 1834–7.

17. Whitington, pp. 26–27.

18. Ibid., p. 25.

19. Quoted in Skelly, 'Falklands Story,' p. 10.

20. O'Byrne, pp. 1085–1086.

21. Lieut. Henry Smith to Rear-Admiral Seymour, 18 July 1834, Adm. 1/42. Smith to Hamond, 4 May 1835, Adm. 1/44.

22. Note by Hamond, n.d. (1835), Adm. 1/43. Hamond to C. Wood (Adm.), 14 November 1836, Adm. 1/47.

23. Hay to Elliot, 5 August 1834, and Admiralty minute thereon, 6 August 1834, Adm. 1/425. Hay to Backhouse, 19 May

1835, F.O. 6/501. Backhouse to Hay, 29 May 1835, C.O. 78/2. Hay to Wood, 10 August 1835, Adm. 1/4259. See Down, pp. 150–51, for a fine discussion of this question.

24. Ouseley to Palmerston, 29 July 1839 and 9 January 1840, GC/OU/35/2 and GC/OU/42, Broadlands MSS.

25. Remark book of H.M.S. *Blonde*, 1834, R.B. 1834 & 1835, unpaginated, H.D.

26. Grey Diary, 1836, in H.D.; printed in *F.I.J.* 1980, pp. 4–5. His official despatch is reported in Hamond to Wood, 9 March 1837, Adm. 1/49.

27. Hamond to Wood, 9 March 1838, Adm. 1/49.

28. Hamond to Wood, 13 October 1837, Adm. 1/49.

29. Instructions for Lieutenant Robert Lowcay, H.M.S. *Sparrow*, 29 October 1837, Adm. 1/50.

30. Lowcay to Hamond, 19 February 1838, Adm. 1/51, enclosing account of proceedings.

31. Hamond to Wood, 30 October 1837, Adm. 1/50.

32. Lowcay to Hamond, 4 February 1838, Adm. 1/51. John Dodson to Viscount Palmerston, 12 February 1838, no. 80, F.O. 83/2227, pp. 205–205v.

33. Lords of the Admiralty to Rear-Admiral Sir Edward Durnford King, 25 September 1840, Adm. 2/1330, pp. 92–4.

34. As did H.M.S. *Sparrow*, Lieutenant Lowcay, in August 1838.

35. Quoted in S. Miller, 'American Sealers in the Mid-Nineteenth Century,' *F.I.J.*, 1980, p. 29, which demonstrates that American depredations continued despite British sovereignty being clearly displayed.

36. Hamond to Wood, 20 June 1836, Adm. 1/46. Hamond complained that he had at his disposal only three ships, including the flagship, on the Atlantic side of his station.

37. Hamond Journal, 1837, HAM/127, pp. 202, 267, 276, N.M.M. Also, R. Lowcay, *Tour of the Falkland Islands*, R.B. 1836–37, H.D.

38. Mackinnon, p. 69.

39. Sulivan, 'Climate and Soil of the Falkland Islands,' 5, 10 (1841): 649–55. Also, *Life and Letters of the Late Admiral Sir Bartholomew James Sulivan, 1810–1890*, ed. H.N. Sulivan, with an introduction by Admiral Sir G.H. Richards

(London: J. Murray, 1896), pp. 400–402, and *Derrotero de las islas Malvinas* (Santiago, Chile: Imprenta nacional, 1882).

40. Colonial Land and Emigration Office to J. Stephen, 22 August 1840, encl. in Stephen to Sir John Barrow, 4 September 1840, Adm. 1/5500.
41. Ibid.
42. Ibid.
43. Ibid.
44. Ibid.
45. Admiralty Minute (undated), on Stephen to Barrow, 4 September 1841, ibid. The full estimates for the establishment of the Falklands colony are to be found in *P.P.*, 1841, vol. 14 (224 v).
46. Precis of Moody's report, 7 March 1842, C.O. 714/54 (Index 18512). Sir H. Henniker-Heaton, 'Early Settlement of the Falkland Islands', (1923), reprinted in *F.I.J.*, 1980, p. 35.
47. Lord John Russell to Lieutenant-Governor R.C. Moody, 23 August 1841, *Correspondence Relative to the Falkland Islands*, printed 22 June 1843.
48. Ibid.
49. Ibid.
50. Moody to Lord Stanley, 14 April 1842, copy Adm. 7/705.
51. Ibid.
52. FitzRoy to Beaufort, 30 June 1837, F. 177, H.D.
53. Moody to Lord Stanley, 5 March 1842, ibid. See also, Boyson, p. 114. Sir James Clark Ross, *A Voyage of Discovery ... 1839–43* (2 vols.; London: John Murray, 1847), 2: 257–61.
54. 6 & 7 Vict. c. 13. The statute bore the preamble: 'Whereas divers of Her Majesty's subjects have resorted to and taken up abode at diverse places on or adjacent to the coast of the Continent of Africa and on the Falkland Islands. . . .' The reference to Africa is no mistake: the judicial links and naval authority, including admiralty courts, in some cases being joined as much to Cape Colony and the West African station as to the South American station. On the legal particularities of this and other British attempts to establish effective jurisdictions over sparsely-settled areas, see W. Ross Johnston, *Sovereignty and Protection: A Study of British Jurisdictional*

*Imperialism in the late Nineteenth Century* (Durham, N.C.: Duke University Press, 1973), pp. 49–52, 113. Moody was appointed Lieutenant-Governor 2 August 1841, and installed as such 22 January 1842. He became Governor and Commander-in-Chief by letters patent 23 June 1843 and Admiral of the Islands in September.

55. Ninth General Report of the Colonial and Emigration Commissioners, 1849 (1082), *P.P.*, vol. XXII, p. 27. H. Merivale (C.O.) to Secretary of the Admiralty, 24 November 1856, Adm. 1/5678.

56. Moody's report, 1842, is in C.O. 78/5. See also 'Falkland Islands Correspondence, since August 1841,' in *P.P.*, 1843, vol 33 (160). 23 & 24 Vict. (1860), cap. 121 amending 6 & 7 Vict. c. 13.

57. *Twelfth General Report of the Colonial Land and Emigration Commissioners, 1852* (1499), *P.P.*, vol. VIII, Appendix, pp. 225–231, esp. summary (p. 231).

58. Papers Relative to the Falkland Islands Company, Shipping, Marts and Guano, etc., *P.P.*, 1852 (1499) vol. 18, giving an excerpt of the *Twelth Report of the Colonial Land and Emigration Commissioner*, pp. 65–7; also Appendix, ibid., p. 225.

59. *Twelfth General Report of the Colonial Land and Emigration Commissioners*, p. 66. The statistical basis for this optimistic view is to be found in Appendix to the Report, pp. 225–31.

60. Quoted in Boyson, p. 122.

61. John Macgillivray, *Narrative of the Voyage of H.M.S. Rattlesnake commanded by the late Captain Owen Stanley. . . . 1846–50* (2 vols.; London: T. & W. Boone, 1852), 2: 99–100.

## Chapter 7: South Atlantic Empire and Diplomacy

1. Williams, *British Commercial Policy*, p. 85, and Gerald S. Graham, *The China Station: War and Diplomacy, 1830–1860* (Oxford: Clarendon Press, 1978), pp. 102–103.

2. Lord Melbourne to Lord Howick, 16 December 1837, Third Earl Grey Papers, Melbourne 115/1, Durham, Durham University Library, quoted in Peter Adams, *Fatal Necessity; British Intervention in New Zealand, 1830–1847* (Auckland: Auckland University Press, 1977), p. 101. The

reluctance of the British to expand in other places is the subject of several studies, including John S. Galbraith, *Reluctant Empire: British Policy on the South African Frontier, 1834–1854* (Berkeley and Los Angeles: University of California Press, 1963) and Ronald Robinson and John Gallagher with Alice Denny, *Africa and the Victorians: The Official Mind of Imperialism* (London: Macmillan, 1961).

3. Quoted in James Morris, *Pax Britannica: The Climax of an Empire* (Harmondsworth, Middlesex: Penguin Books, 1979), p. 429.

4. Hansard, *Parliamentary Debates* (Commons), 25 July 1848. When Molesworth later became Secretary of State for the Colonies he took no measures to implement his 1848 view.

5. Boyson, pp. 111–12, quoting *Fisher's Colonial Magazine*, 1844, i, 608.

6. Whitington, p. 4.

7. Onslow to Whitington, 7 March 1840, Yarmouth, ibid., p. 49.

8. Here I exclude the Falkland Islands Dependencies which though administratively attached to Port Stanley for convenience are separately constituted. See Robert Headland, *The Island of South Georgia* (Cambridge: Cambridge University Press, 1984), pp. 239–42.

9. Destéfani, *The Malvinas*, p. 5.

10. Ibid.

11. Message of the Government on the Opening of the Legislature of the Province of Buenos Ayres, 31 May 1833, in *B.F.S.P.*, 20: 1153–54; exchange of notes between Philip Gore, British charge d'affairs, and Manuel Vincente de Maza, minister of foreign affairs, of January 1833, ibid., pp. 1198–9; Palmerston's reply to Don Manuel Moreno's protest, 8 January 1834, ibid., 22: 1384–94; and Message of the President in the Opening of the Legislature of the Province of Buenos Ayres, 31 December 1835, ibid., 23: 193.

12. Moreno to Aberdeen, 18 December 1841, ibid., 31: 103. Aberdeen to Moreno, 29 December 1841, ibid., p. 1005.

13. This caused *The Times* (14 April 1849) to complain: 'we do not know which to admire most, the impudence of the South American or the self-denial of the Queen's Minister in

not kicking him downstairs' (quoted in Lynch, *Argentine Dictator*, pp. 289–90).

14. For a thorough review of the recent developments in international law and history, to date of publication, see Hoffmann and Hoffmann, *Sovereignty in Dispute*. The key documents are to be found in Perl, *Falkland Islands Dispute*.

15. Moore, p. 889.

16. Quoted in ibid., p 890. The continuity of U.S. policy is demonstrated in Peterson, *Argentina and the United States*, pp. 106–120.

17. *A.R.*, 1982, p. 7.

18. Quoted in Gaston de Bernhardt, Memorandum Respecting the Falkland Islands, Confidential, 7 Dec. 1910, printed (9755), F.O. 371/824/44753, p. 41.

19. Quoted in ibid., pp. 41–42.

20. Ibid, p. 42.

21. In the words of the memorandum (ibid.).

22. Ibid., p. 43.

23. Ibid., p. 45.

24. Ibid.

25. Ibid., p. 45.

26. Ibid, p. 46.

27. The arguments are given at ibid., pp. 46–47.

28. Ibid., p. 48.

29. Ibid., p. 49.

30. Ibid.

31. W. Townley to E. Grey, 5 October 1910, F.O. 371/824/40397.

32. Ibid.

33. In F.O. 371/824/44753, printed January 1911.

34. Minute of Gerald Spicer, 12 December 1910, on Bernhardt's Memorandum Respecting the Falkland Islands, ibid.

35. Ibid.

## Chapter 8: Unfinished Business

1. Charles P. Lucas, *A Historical Geography of the British Colonies, Volume II: The West Indies* (2nd ed.: Oxford: Clarendon Press, 1905), p. 329.

2. Hugh Gunn, ed., *The British Empire* (12 vols.: London: Collins, 1924): 1: 415.

3. William S. Bruce, 'The Falkland Islands and Their Dependencies,' in *The Oxford Survey of the British Empire: America* (Oxford: Clarendon. 1914), p. 448. The population figures as given are provided by Bruce from colonial reports.

4. An Ordinance to Regulate the Whale Fishery of the Colony of the Falkland Islands, *Falkland Islands Gazette*, for 1 August 1908, vol. 18, no. 8, pp 101–103. This tougher measure replaced a previous ordinance for 1906.

5. *Falkland Islands Gazette*, 1 September 1908, vol. 18, no. 9, pp. 106–108; also *B.F.S.P.*, 1907–08, vol. 101, pp. 76–77.

6. Ordinance to Regulate the Whale Fishery of the Colonies, ibid., pp. 115–17.

7. For discussion, see *International Court of Justice Pleadings, Antarctica Cases (United Kingdom v. Argentina; Kingdom v. Chile)* (1956), p. 61.

8. L. Harrison Matthews, *South Georgia: The British Empire's Subantarctic Outpost* (Bristol: John Wright, 1931), p. 132.

9. Ibid. This was learned by L. Harrison Matthews in his discussions with Norwegians in the 1902s. As one scholar points out, Hodges' action was 'a matter omitted from the log book and official report.' A.G.E. Jones, 'Three British Naval Antarctic Voyages, 1906–43,' *F.I.J.*, 1981, pp. 29–36. I have not seen Captain Hodges' report of 11 February 1906 to Governor Allardyce on this episode; details and extracts are in Headland, *Island of South Georgia*, p. 67, also cited in FIG Archives, Ser. B30/212, in D.W.H. Walton, 'The First South Georgia Leases, Compañia Argentina de Pesca and the South Georgia Exploring Company Limited,' *F.I.J.* 1983, pp. 22–23.

10. Headland, *South Georgia*, p. 67–68.

11. Ibid., p. 68.

12. See on this the telling second chapter of Robert Falcon Scott, *The Voyage of the Discovery* (2 vols.; London: Smith Elder, 1905).

13. Quoted in Roland Huntford, *Shackleton* (London: Hodder and Stoughton, 1985), p. 27.

14. Ibid.

15. Ordinance, 2 December 1915, in *Falkland Islands Gazette*, vol. 24, no. 13, pp. 167–68.
16. *I.C.J. Pleadings*, p. 62.
17. Letters Patent, 28 March 1917, in *Falkland Islands Gazette*, vol., 26, no. 7, pp. 69–70; also *B.F.S.P.*, 1917–18, vol. 111, pp. 16–17.
18. *I.C.J. Pleadings*, p. 9.
19. For discussion of the boundaries of Argentina's claim, see ibid., pp 9–10.
20. Ibid., p. 24.
21. Ibid.
22. Ibid.
23. Gordon Ireland, *Boundaries, Possessions and Conflicts in South America* (1936; reprint, New York: Octagon Books, 1971), pp. 36–37.
24. *I.J.C. Pleadings*, p. 26.
25. Ibid.
26. Ibid., pp. 26–27.
27. *The Disputed Islands: The Falkland Crisis: A History & Background* (London: H.M.S.O., 1982).
28. Ibid.
29. Ibid.
30. South-American Department, Foreign and Commonwealth Office, [The Shackleton Report] *Economic Survey of the Falkland Islands* (2 vols.; H.M.S.O., 1976).
31. *Disputed Islands*, p. 30.
32. Ibid.
33. Ibid.
34. Ibid., p. 34.
35. Ibid.
36. *Parliamentary Debates* (Hansard), 6th ser., vol. 21 (Sess. 1981–82). pp. 633–34.
37. Perl, *Falkland Islands . . . Documentary Sourcebook*, p. 419.
38. *The Shackleton Report*, 1982, p. 3; quoted in Lord Shackleton, 'Why the Falklands Matter,' *The Times*, 22 April 1985, p. 10.
39. 'Menem Seeks Arbitration on Falklands,' *The Independent*, 7 January 1992.
40. Beck, *Falkland Islands as an International Problem*, p. 192.

# Sources

This section contains a partial, select list of (1) documentary classes and (2) printed collections, followed by a Bibliography, on a subject which is a veritable vortex. It does not include the United States Archives documentation, which, however, is largely printed in Manning and Moore. Nor does it include Argentine archival collections, though the Woodbine Parish papers in both the British Library and the Foreign Office records provide a rich trove. As with the American papers, the main Argentine diplomatic records for the nineteenth century have been reproduced in Spanish and frequently in English translation in several sources including Calliet Bois, Tesler, Groussac and Gómez Langenheim, though they do not approximate in volume of the printed editions of documentation for the 1760–80 era. The principal British published sources are the *British and Foreign State Papers*. Vernet's memorandum is to be found in volume 20 of this series.

The historical literature on the Falklands/Malvinas in extraordinarily extensive. This is demonstrated by the numerous listings of the following bibliographies and guides, to whom the reader is referred for further details: Everette E. Larson, comp., *A Selective Listing of Monographs and Government Documents on the Falkland/Malvinas Islands in the Library of Congress* (Washington, D.C.: Library of Congress, Hispanic Focus, No. 1, 1982), Margaret P.H. Laver, *An Annotated Bibliography of the Falkland Islands and the Falkland Islands Dependencies as Delimited on 3rd March 1962* (Cape Town: University of Cape Town Libraries, 1977),

José Torré Revello, *Bibliographía de las Islas Malvinas: Obras, napas y documentos* (Buenos Aires: Imprenta de la Universidad, 1953), H.G.R. King, *Atlantic Ocean* (Oxford: Clio Press, World Bibliographical Series, 61, 1985), pp. 159-202, and Robert K. Headland, *Chronological List of Antarctic Expeditions and Related Historical Events* (Cambridge: Cambridge University Press, 1989).

I. DOCUMENTS

*Public Record Office, Kew.*

Admiralty Papers
   Adm. 1 (in letters from C-in-Cs and officers), various volumes, esp. vols. 31, 37-51.
   Adm. 2 (out letters and instructions), various volumes.
   Adm. 7/704. S.W. Clayton, "A Short Description of Falkland's Islands, Their Produce, Climate and Natural History."
Foreign Office Papers
   F.O. 118 (Argentina), vols. 1-46 (1824-45), esp. vol 30B (1833).
   F.O. 6 (Argentina), vols. 499-502 (1829-80).
   Various items of documentation in F.O. 128 (Brazil), vols. 132 and 133, (Chile) 51, (Uruguay), vols. 6-9, F.O. 61 (Chile), vols. 23 and 26, and F.O. 97/135 (Falkland Fisheries), 1832-56).
   F.O. 354, vols. 1-4, Woodbine Parish Papers.
   F.O. 371/824/44753. Memorandum, 1910, by G. de Bernhardt
Colonial Office Papers
   C.O. 78, vols. 1-20 (1829-48) and 43 (Vernet's case).
   C.O. 81/1-5. Falkland Islands.
   C.O. 380/78 and 399/2, Commissions and instructions.
   C.O. 714/54 (Index 18512).

*Historical Manuscripts Commission, Quality Court, Chancery Lane, London*
   Palmerston Papers, Broadlands MSS. Correspondence with consuls, cabinet ministers, and undersecretaries. Moreno letters to Sir G. Shee.

*British Library, London*
> Papers of the Earl of Aberdeen, Add. MSS., Various volumes.
> James Colnett, Journal 1793–94, Add. MSS. 30369.
> Woodbine Parish Collections (1830) of Argentine Documents, Add. MSS. 32603–9.

*Hydrographic Department, Ministry of Defence (Navy), Taunton, Somerset*
> Beaufort Correspondence and General Index
> Remark Books, various
> Captain and Hon. George Grey's diary
> Plans and Charts

*National Maritime Museum, Greenwich*
> Journal of Sir Graham Eden Hamond


2. PRINTED SOURCES

*Annual Register*, various years
*British and Foreign State Papers*, ed. Sir Lewis Herslet (London, 1818–), esp vols. 20, 22 and 23.
*Falkland Islands Gazette*
Gómez Langenheim, A., comp. *Elementos para la Historia de Nuestras Islas Malvinas*. 3 vols.; Buenos Aires: El Ateneo, 1939.
*International Court of Justice Pleadings, Antarctica Cases (United Kingdom v. Argentina; United Kingdom v. Chile)*. (Hague: I.J.C., 1956.
Manning, William R. *Diplomatic Correspondence . . . vol. 1: Argentina*. Washington D.C., 1932.
Moore, John B. *A Digest of International Law*, volume 1. Washington D.C., 1906.
*Parliamentary Papers*, various volumes of correspondence; also estimates and annual reports of Colonial Land and Emigration Commissioners.
*Papers Relative to the Late Negotiation with Spain and the Taking of Falkland's Island*. London, 1777.
Perl, Raphael, comp. *The Falkland Islands Dispute in International Law and Politics: A Documentary Sourcebook*. New York, London and Rome: Oceana Publications, 1983.

# Bibliography

*Account of the Settlement of the Malouines (or Falkland Islands) by the French, in 1763; and also a Voyage round the World . . . 1766, 7, 8, 9 by L. Bougainville*, extract from trans. J.G. Forster, London, 1771.

Allardyce, William L. *The Story of the Falkland Islands . . . 1500-1842*. Letchworth, Herts.: Garden City Press, 1915.

Alonso, Manuel Moreno, 'Las ilas del Atlántico Sur y el imperialismo británico en siglo XIX,' *Annuario de Estudios Americanos*, XL (1983): 313-45.

Andrews, Kenneth R. *Trade, Plunder and Settlement: Maritime Enterprise and the Genesis of the British Empire, 1480-1630*. Cambridge: Cambridge University Press, 1984.

Arce, José. *Las Malvinas (las pequeñas islas que nos fueron arrebatadas)*. Madrid: Instituto de Cultura Hispánica, 1950.

Azpiri, José L.M. *Historia Completa de Las Malvinas*, 3 vols.; Buenos Aires: Editorial Oriente, 1966.

Beck, Peter J. *The Falkland Islands as an International Problem*. London: Routledge, 1988.

Boyson, V.F. *The Falkland Islands, With Notes on the Natural History* by Rupert Vallentin. Oxford: Clarendon Press, 1924.

Caillet-Bois, Ricardo R. *Una tierra argentina. Las Islas Malvinas. Ensayo basado en una nueva y desconocida documentación*. 2d. ed. Buenos Aires: Ediciones Peuser, 1952 (1st ed. 1948).

Calvert, Peter. "Sovereignty and the Falkland Crisis," *'International Affairs*, 59, 3 (Summer 1983): 405-13.

Carril, Bonifacio del. *La cuestión de las Malvinas*. Buenos Aires: Emecé Editores, 1982.

Cawkell, M.B.R. et al. *The Falkland Islands*. London: Macmillan, 1960.

*Colección de documentos relativos a la historia de las Islas Malvinas*. Vol. 1 Buenos Aires: Frigerio Artes Gráficas, 1957. Vols 2 and 3 in one volume. Buenos Aires: Guillermo Kraft Ltda., 1961.

Destéfani, Rear-Admiral Laurio H. *The Malvinas, The South Georgias and The South Sandwich Islands: The Conflict with Britain*. Buenos Aires: Edipress S.A. 1982.

Destéfani, Rear-Admiral Laurie H. *Sintesis de la geograpia y la historia de las Islas Malvinas*. Buenos Aires: Centro Nacional de Documentacion e Informacion Educativa, 1982.

Dickens, Paul D. 'The Falkland Islands Dispute between the United States and Argentina,' *H.A.H.R.*, 9, 4 (November 1929): 471–87.

*Disputed Islands; The Falklands Crisis: History & Background*, London: H.M.S.O., 1982.

Down, W.C., 'The Occupation of the Falkland Islands.' Ph.D. thesis, Cambridge University, 1926/27.

Ferns, Henry S. *Britain and Argentina in the Nineteenth Century*. Oxford: Clarendon Press, 1960.

Fitte, Ernesto H. *La agresión norteamericana a las Islas Malvinas. Crónica documental*. Buenos Aires: Emecé Editores, 1966.

Goebel, Julius. *The Struggle of the Falkland Islands, A Study in Legal and Diplomatic History, with a Preface and an Introduction by J.C.J. Metford*. New Haven: Yale University Press, 1982 [original ed. 1927].

Gough, Barry M. 'Sea Power and South America: The Royal Navy's 'Brazils' or South America Station, 1808–1837,' *The American Neptune*, 50, 1 (Winter 1990): 26–34.

Gough, Barry M. 'The British Reoccupation and Colonization of the Falkland Islands or Malvinas, 1832–1843,' *Albion*, 22, 2 (Summer 1990): 261–87.

Groussac, Paul. *Las Islas Malvinas*. Buenos Aires: Comisión Protectora de Bibliotecas Populares, 1936 [Originally published 1909]; also published as *Les Isles Malvinas* in Anales de la Biblioteca Nacional de Buenos Aires, 1910.

Headland, Robert K. *Chronological List of Antarctic Expeditions and Related Historical Events*. Cambridge University Press, 1989.

Hidalgo Nieto, Manuel. *La cuestión de las Malvinas. Contribución al estudio de las relaciones hispano-inglesas en el siglo XVIII*. Madrid: Consejo Superior de Investigaciones Cietníficas, 1947.

Hoffman, Fritz L. and Olga Mingo Hoffmann. *Sovereignty in Dispute. The Falklands/Malvinas 1493-1982*. Boulder: Westview, 1984.

*International Affairs*, special issue 'Falklands Retrospective,' 59, 3 (Summer 1983).

Izaguirre, Mario. *Estado actual de las cuestión Malvinas*. Buenos Aires: Centro Naval, Instituto de Publicaciones Navales, 1972.

Johnson, Samuel. *Thoughts on the Late Transactions Respecting Falkland's Islands*. London: Printed for T. Cadell, 1771.

Liss, Peggy K. *Atlantic Empires: The Network of Trade and Revolution, 1813-26* Baltimore: John Hopkins University Press: 1983.

Matthews, Leonard Harrison. *South Georgia: The British Empire's Subantarctic Outpost*. Bristol: John Wright and Sons, 1931.

Metford, J.C.J. "Falklands or Malvinas? The Background to the Dispute," *International Affairs*, 44, 3 (Summer 1968): 463-81.

Moreno, Juan Carlos. *Nuestras Malvinas. La Antártida*. Buenos Aires: Cantiello y Cia., 1938.

*La recuperación de las Malvinas*. Buenos Aires: Plus Ultra, 1973.

Muñoz Azpiri, José Luis, *Historia completa de las Malvinas*. 3 vols. Buenos Aires: Editorial Oriente, 1966.

Pereyra, Ezequiel Federico. *Las Islas Malvinas, soberania argentina: antecedentes, gestiones diplomáticas*. Buenos Aires: Secretaria de Estado de Cultura y Educación, 1969.

Peterson, Harold F. *Argentina and the United States, 1810-1960*. New York: State University of New York Press, 1964.

Platt, D.C.M. *Finance, Trade, and Politics in British Foreign Policy, 1815-1914*. Oxford: Clarendon Press, 1968.

Quesada, Héctor C. *Las Malvinas son argentinas (Recopilación de antecedentes)*. Buenos Aires: Secretaria de Educación de la Nación, Sub-secretaria de Cultura, 1948.

Rock, David. *Argentina, 1516-1982: From Spanish Colonization to the Falklands War*. Berkeley and Los Angeles: University of California Press, 1985.

Tesler, Mario. *Malvinas: Como EE.UU. Proroco la Usurpacion Inglesa*. Buenos Aires: Editorial Galerna. 1979.

Thiéry, Maurice. *Bougainville, Soldier and Sailor.* trans. Anne Agnew. London: Grayson and Grayson, 1932.

Tracy, Nicholas. 'The Falklands Islands Crisis of 1770: Use of Naval Force,' *English Historical Review*, 90 (January 1975): 40–75.

Whitington, G.T. *The Falkland Islands* . . . London, 1840.

Williams, Glyndwr. '"The Inexhaustible Fountain of Gold": English Projects and Ventures in the South Seas, 1670–1750,' in John E. Flint and Glyndwr Williams, eds., *Perspectives of Empire: Essays Presented to Gerald S. Graham*, London: Longman, 1973, pp. 27–53.

# Index